BEYOND THE STARTUP

SPARKING OPERATIONAL INNOVATIONS
FOR GLOBAL GROWTH

RALF SPECHT

Radius Book Group

New York

Distributed by Radius Book Group
A Division of Diversion Publishing Corp.
New York, NY
www.RadiusBookGroup.com

Copyright © 2022 by Ralf Specht

All rights reserved, including the right to reproduce this book or portions thereof in any form whatsoever. No part of this publication may be reproduced or transmitted in any form or by any means, electronic or mechanical, including photocopying, recording, or any other means of information storage and retrieval, without the written permission of the author.

For more information, email info@radiusbookgroup.com.

First edition: May 2022
Hardcover ISBN: 978-1-63576-900-5
eBook ISBN: 978-1-63576-901-2

Library of Congress Control Number: 2020901885
Printed and bound in Great Britain by Clays Ltd, Elcograf S.p.A.
10 9 8 7 6 5 4 3 2 1

Cover design by Charles Hames based on a concept from Lee Aldridge
Interior design by Neuwirth & Associates, Inc.

Radius Book Group and the Radius Book Group colophon are registered trademarks of Radius Book Group, a Division of Diversion Publishing Corp.

I dedicate this book to my two sons:

Till and Ivo.

Now you know in detail what has kept your dad busy over the past nine years.

*It is to you, dear entrepreneur,
that I dedicate these pages in the hope that you will find in them
inspiration, practicality, and a good idea or two.*

If you want to go fast, go alone
If you want to go *far*, go together

—South African proverb

CONTENTS

Foreword by Ian Armstrong vii

Start Me Up xi

1. **The Entrepreneur as Global Chief Executive**
   An Awareness of What It Means to Let Go and Lead 1

2. **The Working Value System**
   How to Create a Belief System that Is
   Meaningful and Actionable 15

3. **A Place at the Table**
   How to Build an Interdependent Skills
   and Personality-Based Management Team 33

4. **Talent Centricity**
   Twenty-First Century Human Resources 46

5. **Evolving the Client Marriage**
   How to Adapt to Ever-Changing Customers 63

6. **Taking Advantage of a Good Crisis**
   How a Crisis Becomes a Means to Propel
   the Company to the Next Stage 73

7. **Follow the Money**
   Building New Kinds of Customer-Focused Incentives 83

8. **Managing Globally**
   Creating an Interdependent Organization 96

9. **Expanding Your Footprint**
   Establishing New Locations, Going Global,
   and Yet Keeping Your Soul 109

10. **Creating Your Legacy**
    Understanding What You're Building,
    What You're Leaving, and Your Exit Strategy by
    Reflecting on the Four Typologies of "Leavers" 126

Afterword: It's All About the People
They Made and Make the Difference 137

Acknowledgments
There Is No Business Without a Client 141
Rest in Peace 143

Great Readings
Inspiration and Direction Are Often
Found in Special Places 145

FOREWORD

BY IAN ARMSTRONG

"We've got a big plan," they said. "Have you ever worked with a joint venture advertising agency? We've just created our own. It's about eighty people but will grow to over eight hundred in eighteen markets in the next five years. We need to double the size of the business, more than triple the product line, and improve profitability dramatically."

A few minutes pass, and I reply, "Okay."

And so it began. In January 2012, as global head of advertising for Jaguar, I began working with Spark44, which was only a few months old. Spark44 was already making a significant impact on the Jaguar's business, and not for all positive reasons, either. Local offices were now being told, "We're going to do things differently from now on," which diminished their control, budget autonomy, and ability to make their own decisions. This was a real test for someone in my position, striving for strategic and tactical alignment globally, especially when I shared more than just the intent and motivation to succeed, but I shared the discomfort of being perceived to be on the "agency" side by my local colleagues.

There were some defining characteristics about such a young business, including the dream and vision of changing fundamentally how the business is run, as well as the conviction and belief that you're right and the drive to invest the time and energy to make the change on the ground in every team and every market. The energy and belief of building a new model that will ultimately change how the business will work are powerful. In my case, I was lucky enough to be at the center of that crucible. I was involved in a partnership that was designed and created to bring about change and deliver superior work that would convince new buyers in new segments and new markets.

As a client who has run a number of agency selection pitch processes in my career, I've noticed a pattern that emerges in appointing new agency partners; you see the founders of the business for all of the initial meetings and the early days of the relationship and over time they recede into the upper floors of the agency only to be seen at key moments or seasonal events. The challenge is, how do you create a culture in an organization that endures well beyond the initial honeymoon? What's interesting about Spark44 is that the senior leaders were always present, involved in a range of decisions and discussions. This presence had a reinforcing effect on the way the culture developed. There was a constant embellishing of the values and principles on which the agency was founded, a constant reminder that this was different and something new. The shared vision was never in doubt; the organization had agreed on a plan and rules of engagement that constantly challenged the status quo.

Combine strong leadership, a jointly developed strategy based on full transparency, and an operational management model designed to share and collaborate, and you can create some real efficiencies around the world. This improves both budgetary performance through the clever use of investment and the resource management efficiency of a self-starting agency, identifying the not-so-obvious gaps in the master plan. These are some of the future foundations that allow the business to transition from a small operationally effective startup into a robust and critical trading partner. A transition not without its challenges, detractors, and hurdles, but when it's based on an enduring, strong belief system and an unwavering leadership approach, you can begin to see the results.

In this remarkable journey the business more than doubled, with the biggest lineup of products in Jaguar's history and the addition of Land Rover to the stable, supported by an agency model grown from a strong vision and commitment to make it work on both sides at very senior levels. You begin to see fruits of your labors when you combine this with a focus on quality output and industry-breaking work. Jaguar's first global Effie for the British Villains campaign and

Land Rover's first Effie for China's Dragon Challenge are testaments to a combined team working hard together to deliver world-beating work in a highly competitive segment.

On reflection, having left Jaguar Land Rover, I knew Spark44 was always going to be a challenge to its own team and that of Jaguar and Land Rover. You can't create a single P&L agency supporting every market in the world and expect the world to open its arms to the agency as a utopian solution to all their problems. The test therefore becomes whether the approach can make a difference, whether it can produce the quality required to change hearts and minds of new customers, and whether it can deliver innovative ways for companies to work together and deliver results. The Spark44 joint venture pushed many boundaries both in the Jaguar / Land Rover business and in the wider agency community by operating a new model of engagement where reward and success were dependent on both parties working together. It's a testament to the whole team involved that the business enjoys the success it does today.

They said it was new and innovative; it was. They said it would be challenging; it was. They said it would deliver results; it did.

IAN ARMSTRONG

Global Head of Advertising, Jaguar & Land Rover 2014–2018
Global Marketing Communications Director, Jaguar 2012–2014

START ME UP

I started my professional career in the publishing industry with Bertelsmann back in 1984. While my interest in fiction and nonfiction had been strong then, never did I think I would write a book. There are so many things you don't think can happen when you start—but they happen when the time has come.

Likewise, there are so many unknowns when you are involved with a startup. Both at the time of starting up and at the time when you take the enterprise to scale. As I write these lines, nine years have passed since we got started.

This book is about sparking innovations for global growth. When we started, we never thought we would become a company of the size we became. This book is about the many things that allowed us to become that company while keeping our soul.

Throughout my career I had the enormous privilege to work with outstanding leaders who taught me many things: Dick Robertson, who taught me how to operate in an international environment. Gunnar Wilmot, who could see through things and cut to the chase every time but always made sure that the individual in front of him got the respect they deserved. Chris Weil, for whom culture has always been the starting point, which still shows in his business today.

But with the inception of Spark44 I had the honor to work with an individual whose talent and skill was paired with a level of personal integrity that is second to none. Hans Riedel, our first chairman, who became a legend in the premium automotive world, was that person. Hans's unparalleled passion, his huge wisdom and knowledge about both the marketing and brand side as well as the key levers in organizational design and the drivers within global sales teams, made him an invaluable partner in managing our agency. He became chairman of Spark44 on day one and remained in that position until December 2017; he has become a true friend over these years and his thoughts have always been enriching. When we got slightly off base, he ensured we came back; when we had "the sky is the limit" plans, he was there to help make them a reality.

And there is Kevin Allen, without whom this book would not have happened. Many times during our collaboration he said, "Ralf, you've got to write a book about this." Sometime in the autumn of 2018 I was convinced. The journey started.

Starting up brings many sacrifices to your private life. For some that have never worked in such an environment, these sacrifices are hard to believe or even understand. I am very happy that my wife Maria lived through many of the ups and downs that I experienced over the "Spark44 Years"; her sense of "what is the right thing here" was typical for many Friday evening conversations when we were sharing what good—or not-so-good—things had happened during the course of the last week.

From the bottom of my heart to all of you: thank you.

CHAPTER 1

THE ENTREPRENEUR AS GLOBAL CHIEF EXECUTIVE

AN AWARENESS OF WHAT IT MEANS TO LET GO AND LEAD

"Steve . . . I'm in."

It was an October evening in Frankfurt, 2010. I had just gotten home from work, after having spent a week in San Francisco at the McCann WorldGroup conference that was supposed to motivate the worldwide leadership team regarding the new CEO who had just taken over and was sharing his agenda to take the company into the next decade.

All of a sudden, my phone buzzed. I could not believe who was calling. "Steve Woolford—Los Angeles" was the name on the display. We had not spoken for quite a while. Six years before, we gotten to know each other well. Steve was running Zentropy Partners, McCann's digital agency, and I was in charge of the European General Motors account at McCann Europe. We worked very closely together to save the agency from losing the entire website business to intruders from outside. We succeeded, and the business continues to flourish to this day. We bonded over the experience.

I thought it was rather surprising for a Thursday night, thinking to myself, *why the earth would he be calling?* I answered, and the characteristic enthusiasm of Steve could be heard. The conversation went sort of like this . . .

"Ralf!"

"Steve, long time! How are you?"

"Are you sitting down?"

"Steve, what's up?"

"Well, I am involved in a consulting project with Jaguar Land Rover through my old boss Hans Riedel. Let me give you the headline: They want to form an advertising agency in a 50-50 joint partnership and asked me to put together the best car folks in the world to be the other half of the partnership; so, I am putting together a radically new agency model for them and I believe you would be the ideal founding partner! Are you game?"

Now, knowing Steve so well, a man with vision, sheer endless energy, overflowing enthusiasm, and optimism—which I balanced with my sense of reality—I wasn't sure whether this was real or if he was having one of his moments.

"Steve, this sounds too good to be true. Feels like this could be the agency model that we always envisioned when we were going through those tough times with GM. But—sounds too good to be true. Do you have a business model?"

"Yes, I got the commercials drafted in a spreadsheet and thought you might give it a shot too."

"Send it over—I'll look at it over the weekend."

The next day Steve's email with the business model arrived. Scrutinizing the logic and reviewing every number, I thought, "This could really work." I called him the same evening:

"Steve . . . I'm in."

It was one of those life-changing moments. A rare moment in my life where I deliberated about career and life decisions with some level of scrutiny. Upon reading the material, it took me not even a minute to commit myself to Spark44. For the next few weeks, Steve and I chatted daily.

We had a dynamic vision to create a global marketing communications company, one built entirely on the foundations of twenty-first-century organizational design and operating methodology. Little did any of us know then that from this wild idea, a nineteen-office, thousand-person-strong multinational, multi-award-winning marketing communications company would propel both the Jaguar and Land Rover brands through creating some of the most memorable and effective advertising the industry had seen in decades.

A NOBLE EXPERIMENT

Apart from the sheer business challenge, what struck me most about the opportunity was, by virtue of having an instantaneous customer foundation in Jaguar and subsequently Land Rover, we would go from the humblest of beginnings as a fledgling startup to the establishment of a global presence with everything that entailed, in record time. We would have the opportunity to put in place, in all corners of the company, the most contemporary, advanced, twenty-first-century means of building and running a multinational organization. We would not be hampered in any way by lack of demand for our products and services or the distractions of early growth or old operating legacy. We could focus on the construction of a contemporary global company, rejecting existing modes of creating management teams, internal communication, human resource practices, and even operations and financial controls. We would break every rule in the book.

Not Everything Is Just Upside
Before you can break every rule, you obviously need to become a real company—in our case that required the approval of JLR and the Tata Board. Any board that approves investment decisions wants to see a risk assessment as well as a view of the opportunity. The latter was simple: you only get to the board approval when you have sponsors that weigh in with you on the opportunity. But a risk assessment is different—now you need to put yourself into the shoes of your business partners and conduct a thorough analysis about the risk impact your business will create.

While starting from scratch allows you to paint on a white sheet of canvas, it also brings with it several significant liabilities, because—let's face it—your plans and aspirations might be big, but the execution might not be as easy and simple as you think. A significant commercial risk is involved in setting up a global company from scratch.

Discussing the risks of our endeavor was an eye-opening discussion for all involved—an exercise that I recommend not only for anyone who is starting a new company but also for those at later stages of the journey when they are scaling up.

Years later, we looked at the risks we identified then and realized that they had not come to pass because we were fully aware of them and managed the company with consciousness of them. As the company grows, keeping an eye on the potential risks of any commercial decision becomes a huge responsibility for management.

Lessons for a Growth Aspirant

Reflecting one afternoon with my good friend and former McCann Erickson colleague Kevin Allen, it occurred to us both that there were dozens upon dozens of companies who were reaching the point of going global and expanding their successful startup beyond their original boundaries. Having curated a thriving twenty-first-century global startup in Spark44, it occurred to me that not only did I have a story to tell, but also that I could share many lessons that founders and executives would find both inspiration and consummately practical in growing their companies beyond their original scope. I was inspired to tell the story of the development of Spark44, a most unconventional company, and of the practices that we developed, the means of running the company that we engineered, and the setbacks we endured, all as a way of helping entrepreneurial companies take that next extraordinary leap.

Maintaining the Spirit

Scaling a company is quite a feat when you are graduating from successful startup to a much larger, multinational enterprise. Success for you will not come from following the patterns and practices of existing companies simply because they happen to be large firms; success will come as you leapfrog over old and, in many cases, outdated practices, effectively building yourself a twenty-first-century organization. You are making a key transition, from founder, hands-on creator, and innovator, to inspirer, communicator, and champion of a community of like-minded people driven by a deep set of values and an abiding spirit. The transformation you are making, one we experienced, involves not putting aside entrepreneurial behaviors for more corporate, or "big league," behavior, but rather ensuring that the elements of creativity, innovation, a can-do spirit, and customer-centricity stay with you and are spread far and wide. At the same time, the transformation involves building the right tools, practices, and behaviors that will help you scale successfully. Essentially you are creating a following, enlisting people to your founding principles and beliefs, with the spirit you brought to creating the company in the first place. You'll also want to nurture those in your organization who have this spirit and make sure that they act as role models in the organization, because they're your gold mine.

SECOND GENERATION

Although I was at the center of creating and building this company, I am actually the second-generation chief executive. The first generation was Steven Woolford, the man who had the founding idea and invited me to join his team because he felt, from the experience we had previously, that I had a similar entrepreneurial spirit. We were like-minded, and we had complementary skills. In so many ways Steve embodied the first phase of creating this amazing enterprise, and I, as his fortunate successor, represented the company well beyond the startup.

I had a very charismatic chief executive in Steve, and because he was the founder of the whole thing, he was the guy that everybody looked to. He was the guy without whom this wouldn't ever have been established, so credit goes to him in this regard. I was the chief operating officer for six years, so I knew the company inside and out. I didn't fully realize in the beginning how different the two jobs are. As a global chief operating officer, you're making sure that everything works the way it's supposed to work, and you connect the dots that need to be connected. Chief executive—well that's another kettle of fish. For many entrepreneurs, I think, there is a profound transition from the hands-on, nitty-gritty of the business—which very much described my role as COO—to the values-driven, vision-oriented, hands-off role of a true CEO. For many, including me, it was quite a transition.

Be Yourself
One of the things you might be thinking is that moving into this new transformative phase of your development means a transformed you. Not so. While you will certainly need to adopt new skills and adapt to a new role, the very best thing—in fact the *only* thing—you can be is your own true self. People have followed you for the person you are, and they will continue to do so, provided you don't, in an effort to be more "Global CEO," become someone you're not. To do so is to lose touch with your following. I was challenged with being myself, finding my "voice." Steve and I were brothers in mind, but his way of expressing himself and my way of expressing myself couldn't be any more different. He was very emotional; he was very passionate and very much the communicator. I was calm, considered, thoughtful, perhaps a man of fewer words than he. While initially I had my doubts about how I would connect with the team as CEO, what I learned later was that while my style was much more reserved than Steve's, people saw and felt as much passion, belief, and vision from me as they did from Steve. It was just a question of embracing my own style and delivering my natural voice. Believe me, if you want to be Jeff Bezos, forget about it; and if you want to be Steve Jobs, forget about that, too; you are who you are, and your credibility comes from your own true self.

Watch His Back

As you embark on this new journey, you need to bring your existing people with you and to enlist new ones to travel with you. The only tool you have for this is the power of the spoken word. This is the most important skill you need as you move into an era of managing a company well beyond your ability to touch, feel, and see physically. Steve was clear that he wanted to move on when he hit his sixty-fifth year. Steve and I planned the transition process very carefully. We started the conversation when he was sixty-two, actually three years before it happened. We broke the news to the leadership at one of our annual management meetings—half a year before the changing of the guard. On that day, sixty of our most senior people assembled for our three-day off-site meeting. On the afternoon of day three Steve gave a very passionate and heartwarming speech and, in typical Steve style, made a request of the assembled team: "I have one wish, and that one wish is that you support Ralf as you did me. This is going to be tough. It's going to be tough for you, and for him. He will have to represent you and he will at times need to be tough with our client partners when there's the need to be tough. But he can only be tough if you've got his back. So, do me one favor as my leaving gift: make sure he knows you've got his back, because this only works if it's a team and you're behind him." It was a very emotional moment for all of us.

A Message from Ralf

Then, six months later the day had come. Now it was my turn. The entire company waited to hear my very first words to them. I knew this would in many ways be the most important set of words I had ever put together. So here is lesson number one: rethink what and how you write to your team. If you don't write much . . . start. The bigger your company gets, the more you need to communicate and the more human and "from your voice" your messages need to be. I never understood why, during my corporate life, people communicated with each other as if they were from the IRS. Language is a tool. It's how you reach your people. In the early days of your startup business, you could speak with all your people one-on-one; now, you need to connect with them by the power of the written word.

I labored over my first message for weeks. I wrote and wrote, reviewed, and then threw it all away and started again. I had all kinds of lofty titles, but in the end I entitled it "A message from Ralf." In the end, I asked myself, how do I speak with them now? The final version was based on a simple idea: what I wanted for everyone in the firm. What I wanted them to experience, what I wanted them to achieve, and what I wanted them to be able to celebrate in the years to come. It was not a vision pronouncement. In my message I pledged we would be working together toward an exciting new chapter in the weeks ahead. It was a message from my heart, written as I would speak to them one-to-one. Here is what I wrote:

> Now as your new CEO there are three important questions: What do I believe? What will we do? And what will I do?
>
> Of course, I share deeply the values of being bold, brave, and honest, but there are some other things I believe that some of you may know, but certainly all will come to know:
>
> I believe everyone deserves a place at the table.
>
> Diversity and inclusion are what make a high-performing company. We will be celebrated across the industry for this vitally important cultural requirement.
>
> I believe everyone must be heard.
>
> For good or for bad we will either succeed or fail to the degree to which our people feel free and the mechanisms exist both to innovate but also to critique, to challenge, and to share their views on what may be restricting or supporting progress toward the achievement of greatness.
>
> I believe we must take more risks.
>
> Client service must not be defined as servitude. It must mean challenging our clients and bringing them new and expansive means of advancing their fortunes. It is all about not what is requested but what is required.

I believe we must decentralize innovation.

I want a culture of experimentation where greatness is created not as a top-down affair but in all corners of the company, big or small, and where people feel unfettered permission to create something great.

And what will we do?

In the first week of February the management team will meet to firm up the plan in more detail—what precise steps we will be taking and how it will involve each and every one of you—for if the plan is to be a success it is one which engages the entire company. Let me already today outline the key thoughts:

First—Disruptive Ideas
Creation of groundbreaking disruptive ideas for the JLR brands, leveraging all forms of technological capabilities

Second—New Partnerships
Growth of Spark44 in the formation of new partnerships in new categories

Third—Different Customer Engagement
Leadership in personalized mass communication

Fourth—Enhanced Digitalization
Breakthroughs in new forms of communication beginning with virtual reality and artificial intelligence

Fifth—Continued Efficiency
Leveraging technologies to maintain our competitive edge in efficiency

And finally, what will I do?

There are many ways to define the chief executive's job. My task will be to drive the Recognition of the Greatness. I will be its coach, champion, leader, curator and salesman. For me a contemporary chief executive is a change agent, and I intend to set my sights accordingly. Everything I will do will connect back to our "WHY" — as in empowering people to challenge conventions so that amazing things happen.

I was overwhelmed with the feedback, the most moving of which was the following note:

Hi Ralf

Any change I suppose is accompanied by a nervousness of the unknown and a general feeling of unease ahead of it. I know this has been felt for the past year in various offices around the world.

But your note is inspired, and inspiring. And I think it's exactly what everyone needs to read at exactly the point that they need it.

I hope you don't mind me saying so, since I'm only really a temporary member of the MD's email chain.

And I hope you know that always, you can count on me to support. I joined Spark44 six years ago because I believed in it and it's why I'm still here today.

Finally, I hope that there are plenty of celebration drinks on the cards, because the crazies that drink together are the crazies that stay together. The Brazil office will certainly raise a toast in your honor at our happy hour on Friday!

Nikki

Of course, I was pleased by the outpouring from the forward-leaning folk—that I expected, but what was especially gratifying were the positive sentiments from those I perceived as sitting on the fence. I think this was because they experienced me as their COO and so they expected a lot of process, cost, and structural conversations, but all of a sudden, I was writing to them about being a keeper of our culture.

Sharing Your Vision

Within two minutes of digesting your message, your people will be asking themselves, "Okay, now what?" Employee expectations are, in my experience, unforgiving. I had to walk the walk, because sending out the memo is one thing, but living it out is another. Be seen... get away from your desk as much as you can. You've got to get into every office; you've got to talk to people. Sure, it gets more difficult because you've got less time and there are more people than in the early days when you knew everyone by name, but it is an essential part of your transition to global CEO.

You may be the original founder, or someone like me taking the reins of the firm. No matter what, stating your aims is vital, not once in a while, but often and with passion. I knew people were waiting for me to define my vision and share it with the company. As you move beyond the startup, your goal-setting must be a rallying focus for your people's efforts, and a glue that holds business objectives and strategies together. If you are the originating CEO, what ambition will set your next stage of the company's journey that stands apart from the early days? If you follow a founder, as I did, how is your ambition different from your predecessor's? I defined five core objectives in order to give direction to the company, and, looking back, we achieved some of them in year one, some of them in year two, and some were actually transformational in the sense that if you achieved a key milestone you defined the next step on the way.

Now, these strategies were great, but they were not a vision. What did I want everything to accrue to? What would be our shared vision and focus? As I looked long and hard at where we were, I came to the realization that people had no idea who we were, in spite of our creating a revolutionary agency model, breakthrough, and award-winning marketing communications for Jaguar and Land Rover. I decided to label our vision *The Era of Recognition* because we had been pretty much under the radar. It was time for the world to know what a best-kept secret we were. As we were pursuing business with other clients, that under-the-radar stance was no longer good enough, because if people didn't know us, how could they choose us or select us or want to get into conversations with us? We would still drive to create huge breakthroughs and innovations. This time, though, the world would know about it.

The Steely Gaze

As you'll see in the coming pages, I am a big subscriber to the idea of emotional intelligence and the power of deep-keeled culture. I discovered that these combined instincts would be the means to propel Spark44 to its next stage. The inspiration came from a remarkable fellow, Neil Cassie, who counsels chief executives at major corporations around the world. He said, "Well, you've got the credibility, the whole organization trusts that you will be the one who can bring Spark44 to its next stage of scale successfully, and while you have communicated your vision clearly, the one thing that you haven't communicated to them is that you're dead serious where you intend to go and the changes you're going to make. You've got to show your *steely gaze*." Now, I'm not a steely gaze sort of guy, so I invented my version of it. Mine was holding up a mirror to everyone and giving my people the permission, if you want to put it positively, or the accountability, if you put it a bit more negatively, to deliver. "You are the ones who will do this," I told them. "I will support you, give you the tools, but make no mistake, I will hold *you* accountable." It was a surprise to everybody because they were used to me being about fixing things and getting involved in execution. I was going from "Ralf will sort it all out" to "that's why I have you." The key was remaining authentic. I didn't play a Ralf that I wasn't. I actually gave them the Ralf that I needed to be when the time was right. As every entrepreneur, as every chief executive, and as everybody else for that matter, you've got your doubts, you know where your shortcomings are, you know what you're not good at. My experience is, if you do it the way you are, people understand. They also know exactly who you are and what your strengths are, too. That is, if you let them see.

The Loneliest Person on the Ship

At one time or another I reckon we've all heard someone, probably an ex-CEO, tell us how our lives will change when we are the ultimate decisionmakers, especially in a complex organization, and how the captain sits alone with the weight of the world on his shoulders. I never bought into that either before or after I took the helm of the Spark44 ship (a pirate ship, as our team would often say). I believe in *interdependence*, an interlocking of diverse talent, perspective, and experience. I never felt exposed, unprepared, uninformed, or ill-equipped to face what was thrown at us, in any situation we ever faced. Yes, I did feel the weightiness of my decisions, and the gravitas of being the final decisionmaker, but I never felt alone. *Nor should you.* Surround yourself with energy, diversity, passion, and ability. Your inner circle may make your life crazy at times. If they are the right people, they will challenge you and disagree at times, but you will confront each milestone in the journey confidently, and if you are as lucky as I, have a whole lot of fun along the way.

The Cultural Ambassador

I have always been a big believer in the importance and power of a company's culture, but when I assumed the role of CEO I really came to understand why and saw its power up front. It made me realize how much my role as CEO is to communicate, evangelize, and enlist. The founding principle of the company was to redefine marketing communications services, to be disrupters and innovators. We were on a mission for the Jaguar brand, and we felt that in order to do this, we had to give ourselves a sort of permission, manifested in the concept of *being bold, being brave,* and *being honest.* As you will see a little later, it's easy to write down these values, but it's no easy feat to manage and hold everybody accountable to them. What was more challenging was that I knew the employee concern was how the culture of the company might change. Was it going to be a different culture just because one CEO was the extrovert, and the passionate guy is now giving way to the steady introvert . . . the crazy Californian to the cool German?

Culture and belief system are the most important elements propelling your company toward scale, presence, and greatness. The words that embody what you and your people believe are the glue that binds the citizenship of everyone in your company, guiding you like the North Star toward a noble purpose. They transcend the person in the job. You are its custodian. Your role in this is singular and indivisible. And, so, as a first step in our journey together, may I suggest you rip up your chief executive officer card, and instead reprint as *chief inspiration officer.*

Checking the List	
✓	Is there a can-do, entrepreneurial, and innovative spirit in your company?
✓	Can you distinguish between your role as founder and your role as CEO?
✓	What is your true style?
✓	Do you know who is part of your interdependent team?
✓	Have you crystalized your message to your team as you prepare to expand?

CHAPTER 2

THE WORKING VALUE SYSTEM

HOW TO CREATE A BELIEF SYSTEM THAT IS MEANINGFUL AND ACTIONABLE

"Listen, at the end of the day the real difference, where culture matters, is when it costs money."

"When you're taking those decisions to actually protect the culture even if it costs you. That's where it falls short or where it really shows."

Walk into any one of Spark44's nineteen offices, and you'll be greeted by a mural. The murals are unique to each office, but all are emblazoned with three phrases: *Be Bold, Be Brave, Be Honest.* These phrases encapsulate the belief system of the Spark44 community. They provide a cultural glue, a behavioral divining rod, and the North Star that guides where we are heading as a company. One of the single most important steps in the life of a maturing startup company is the development of meaningful and transcendent values that bind your ever-growing enterprise. In the early stages of your journey, your partners and key employees are the living embodiment of your values. These values are expressed and lived as extensions of your own personal beliefs and how you see your company. Your employees understand, embrace, and reflect the belief system of your firm, simply by watching *you*. The dilemma you face is how to provide an exponentially growing company with a set of values that is meaningful and reflective and transcendent of the founders. The challenge in the early stages of a company's development is values largely lived out instinctively, an outgrowth of individual personalities, rather than a strategically crafted, widely disseminated set of beliefs.

ORIGINS

As in so many early-growth companies, you spend every day working frantically, often with far fewer resources than you feel are needed to do the work. Your to-do list is miles long, with some days prioritized on the basis of "absolutely must do" versus "would be nice to do." For us, the motivation for a codification of values came from seeing initial signs of people going the wrong way. We felt that wasn't what we had intended, but we also felt it wasn't the fault of anyone, because people were trying to do the thing that was right for them in the moment. There wasn't any guideline, or anything to connect with or hold onto other than a few operating principles when we set up the company. One of our initial assertions, which was widely understood by all of our people, was the essential difference the Spark44 joint venture (JV) model afforded clients. It was our twist on an old adage, "You can have good, you can have cheap, you can have fast . . . pick two but you can't have all three." For us, *better, faster, cheaper*, was a great shorthand to remind everyone of how we were going to deliver our work, but it did not give any orientation other than *what* you're doing.

Structurally, we set up the company as a single P&L across the globe and across all subsets of communications disciplines, which were customarily separate at other large communications conglomerates. All of us had experienced multiple P&L environments previously. Often they created a toxic culture in which fighting for money became more important than fighting for the right solution. We did not want this kind of behavior; our focus was to put all the energy into the quality of the output.

By definition, this meant we had set up the company in such a way to leverage complementary skillsets, but all of that only succeeds if people work together. This vital organizational behavior would be under pressure from day-to-day challenges—which could result in people taking a different path because they had to deliver on a client demand of the moment or other business pressures.

Amazing, isn't it, that we in marketing communications can recite chapter and verse about our customers and their businesses, but when it comes to ourselves, the famous adage "The shoemaker's kid is barefoot" applies? Take comfort in the knowledge that you are not alone: distilling the elements of your values—especially if you want them to resonate—is no small task. Whenever I have read accounts of successful companies or famed executives, those stories all somehow seemed to illustrate that the process was the magical, perfectly orderly output of a room full of geniuses. Well, I'll tell you right away, our process bore little resemblance! (Okay, maybe a sprinkling of genius.) So, first, it's perfectly okay for the discussions around your values to be chaotic, and maybe even a little contentious. The most important steps, though, are twofold:

1. To codify a unique and inherent set of values that are genuine in their meaning.
2. To lay out a means to live them out internally—what I call "Working Values."

BE BOLD, BE BRAVE, BE HONEST

The first step we took was to bring together the core people in our firm, and I encourage you to do the same. Not hierarchically speaking, but the people around you who have been vital in shaping the company. Remember, a set of values isn't like those plaques in a conference room no one pays attention to, it's the emotive elements of the human bond, your citizenship. So, by definition, it comes from what you believe, and from the hearts of those who have opted in and shaped your success to date.

Early in our development, we decided we needed the leadership team to meet occasionally face-to-face. We met in our offices but as we grew it became obvious that, in doing so, we would not get enough free headspace for real forward thinking. Staying in offices and hotels does not give you that freedom of mind. So, back in 2015 I asked Simon Moore, who was running our Birmingham office in the British Midlands at the time, to find a place in the UK outside the usual day-to-day work setting, where we would be able to sit back and gauge our progress and "check in" as a management team. He found an old farmhouse in the Cotswolds. No reception, no restaurant, no waiters. Just a cook and us for a good two days. We made huge progress on several topics, and before we departed we all looked at each other and said, "This is it—no more hotel conference rooms ever." We've called the meetings "Finca Meetings" ever since, because farmhouses in Spain are called "fincas" and we all enjoyed the cozy, family-like setting. Being true to ourselves, we called ourselves the "Finca Team." From that day forward, our Finca Meetings became a time out to reflect, check in, and envision our future.

We had already established our values for the company in 2012 when we met in the Los Angeles office. As we were a staff of only 120 at the time, we took the opportunity to ask our people what values they thought would best describe not only what we were going to set up but also what they experienced in their day-to-day lives. Our strategy director led us in a wide-ranging discussion of our vision, mission, market promise, client profile, personality, and values. We were all looking at a series of concentric circles on a huge whiteboard and the conversation got deeper and deeper, more and more complex. The result: a comprehensive and wide-ranging series of concepts and statements describing literally all that could be said of our company, its intention, and its direction. All good, but at one point, one of my colleagues leaned over to me and said, "I think my brain is frying!"

We all took a break and then returned to a heated discussion, when one of the creative directors, Piggy Lines, who was observing more than vocalizing, leaned forward and, in one of those moments when everybody's debating and you can't get to a solution, observed, "Well, wait a second; why don't we make this very simple and call it *be bold, be brave, be honest?"* Dead silence. Our garrulous group sat speechless for a moment, and then Werner Krainz, one of our two creative founding partners, made a remark of the most sublime understatement: "I think that summarizes it rather nicely." Laughter and high-fives ensued.

Amid the complexity, Piggy was able to strip away important but related issues, separate mission and intent and other planning elements, and get to the heart and essential elements of what we all felt, believed, and stood for as the common and profoundly held reason we were all there. When you arrive at a set of words to articulate your values, you won't have to think about it. It will strike you viscerally. For the statement to be reflective of your beliefs it needs to be evocative, not hollow and superficial; simple, not complex; and, above all, expressive of your essential truth. You'll feel it in your gut—and that is exactly what you should trust when arriving at a statement of your beliefs.

Be Honest

Honesty was probably the one value that we zeroed in on first. The founding principle of our company was transparency—and you cannot create transparency without honesty being a core behavior. It would mean and require that our future experience would be a break with the industry's past and present, in terms of compensation and money, cost allocations, or work methods. This was a true partnership—50-50 ownership—which at its core, demanded complete and total transparency. The value of honesty, at a minimum, would require full disclosure, an open-book policy, but it meant much more. It was a way of living, a guiding principle of how we would behave; our obligations to our colleagues and our partners was to be truthful and to share our opinions, especially when difficult topics needed to be discussed that folks might not wish to hear. That's what a true partnership is really all about.

Be Bold

Our employees tell us again and again that one of the most common motivators for joining Spark44 was escaping the "master–servant relationship" the industry had fallen into. With huge competition, margin pressure, and ever-increasing demands, agencies that saw their revenues shrinking sought to please clients at all costs. Boldness, the instinctive desire to create something extraordinary and to make a mark, is, I suppose, at the heart of every marketer and advertising person's desire. We wanted to build our company on a value of boldness, which our partnership structure provides. In a 50-50 partnership, no one is subservient or dominates; you are equals, and the agency's clear province and mandate are to create unfettered brilliance. In effect, it is telling everyone in the firm that confronting conventional wisdom is our job, devoid of politics, compromise, and any external pressures to do otherwise. So, every employee knows that not only is it their job to swing for the fences, but also that they have the backing of everyone in the agency to defend their work to the highest levels of the company. It meant that the senior management team, me included, saw our jobs not as profitmakers, but as brilliant work creators.

Be Brave

If boldness describes the vision to move to a completely new business model, one that stands in contrast to an entire industry, then *bravery* describes fortitude—the fortitude of both joint venture partners to commit to this approach and to, come what may, making it happen. It was the bravery component of our values that gave an impetus, a "what are we going to do about it" quality to our belief system. This provided a "permission" for our people not only to have a bold idea, but also to be encouraged to run with it. Many organizations are in search of how to build a culture of experimentation; it starts first and foremost in creating a climate linked to a value that is *lived*.

Establishing a Working Value System

At first glance, *Bold*, *Brave*, and *Honest* may make you think, "Of course, who doesn't want to be honest? Who doesn't want to be brave for this business? Who doesn't want to create bold work?" It looks so simple, yet it is so difficult in practice, given the various needs in societies and the various interpretations of bold and brave in any culture. We learned that in order to embed a value system into everyday behavior, or to become what I call a *working value system*, we had to make it part of everything we did and "mainstream it" in everyday activity. At its core it is about the following:

1. Conducting a careful and continuous communication of the values and their meaning
2. Embedding these in all aspects of day-to-day operation.
3. Building an accountability system tying back to *be bold, be brave,* and *be honest.*

We began with HR, as this was the focal point for sharing and measuring employee behavior and output. Remember, we wanted to avoid the mistakes that we all felt so bad about when we were working in those multinational holding company driven agencies. Honesty would drive HR and give people an opportunity for reflection and fair challenge about the quality of what they were doing, as well as a bit of coaching and mentoring to improve where people were going. We set up an evaluation system that, in the beginning, we delivered four times a year. As the company grew, we moved it to three times a year, but it was a formal system in which the line manager and the employee discussed what had happened over the past three, four months and evaluated it all in the context of *be bold, be brave,* and *be honest.* The evaluations happened at every level, so the CEO, the receptionist, and everybody in between got a quarterly evaluation. The criteria were the same for everybody, and the payout a score-related percentage of their weekly salary.

Be honest meant you could not treat people at different levels of the organization differently. That's not the culture. We have to treat everybody in a fair way. We initially started with different criteria for each role in the company, in the spirit of *be bold, be brave, be honest,* so the creatives had one set of criteria and the accounting people and finance people had another, and so on. Soon, however, we created the exact same criteria for all, under the banners of boldness, bravery, and honesty and how each employee in their job function acquitted themselves relative to these values. We defined ten behaviors in the context of being bold, brave, and honest, and the whole evaluation focused on how well or poorly employees met these criteria. Whatever your score was, depending on how well you were doing, there was a financial incentive that came with it in order to make sure you understood and acted upon those beliefs, and brought them to life. I think that was probably the breakthrough because, all of a sudden, people realized their behavior really mattered. In other words, connecting the value system with the everyday work at every level is critical.

A PEBBLE IN THE WATER

The pivot point in creating your value system is the moment it starts to become company *culture*. Werner Krainz brought a great deal of wisdom to us founders in one of those conversations about culture. He made a very smart remark: "Listen, at the end of the day the real difference, where culture matters, is when it costs money, when you're taking those decisions to actually protect the culture even if it costs you. That's where it falls short or where it really shows." It was clear that the principle and filter for our evaluation system, compensation, and episodic situations that arose would need to be judged in the context of *be bold, be brave, and be honest*. In the following years, whenever we as a leadership team were confronted with a situation where we had to make a choice, we always reminded ourselves of our values so that the critical choices we made would be credible ones with our employees.

A resonant culture, underpinned by reward and accountability, accelerates its adoption. This is especially true as you move away from the center of the organization. This is the real test: can your values system travel, and how is it supported? Working values travel first by early adopters who seize and articulate them in the context of their office or department.

Years later, our then-leader of the Birmingham office, Emma Forster, observed, "I've got to recognize it beyond the evaluation conversations." So she created the Be Bold, Be Brave, Be Honest Award, which was bestowed for the very first time in 2016. The reception was catalytic. Soon, a ripple effect took hold, with each of our nineteen offices now annually bestowing the Be Bold, Be Brave, Be Honest Award to deserving Spark44 people around the globe.

HIRING AND FIRING

When you're just a few people, it's much easier to establish working values, because you see the behavior. The moment you grow beyond what you can see with your eyes when you're in the office, observing behaviors gets much more challenging. Our largest office, which is in Birmingham, UK, had several leadership changes over the first few years, and we needed to find the right person for the top. We required a person with both great operational skills and a sense of how to manage a large team with a high share of roles that were handled by graduates joining for their first job. We put a team together to do the interviewing, and they came to me and said, "Ralf, we believe we have found the person."

Eschewing the usual capabilities/performance line of questioning, the interview with that person was all about values. I wanted to ascertain *theirs* to see whether that person was capable of representing *ours*. Imagine the reaction when I called the recruiter representing a candidate with the perfect functional resume for the job and said, "Listen, I'm not convinced. We have no alignment on our value systems, I'm sorry." You could literally hear crickets on the other end of the phone. One of our management team, Ahmed Hasan (he was our chief technology officer at the time), had volunteered to be the interim managing director because the previous MD had left, and he said, "Ralf, you know what? It's fine. If they don't reflect who we are and what we believe we'll be right back here soon enough. Let's find the right person and I will stay here until she or he is in place."

We connected with the recruiter again and said, "We've got to go beyond where we've looked so far. Look at their résumés and experience as a given, but screen for our three values: *be bold, be brave, and be honest.*" The recruiter got to work, and a few weeks later we got to a second round of potential candidates. There was this woman from New Zealand who had seen the world and lived and worked in the UK in the US and was currently was working in Amsterdam. She refreshingly aligned with our values and we all felt she was the one who was able to take the office to new heights. The woman, by the way, was Emma Forster. She was able to turn the Birmingham office into the engine room of our global operation within only two years. All websites are managed from there, and the majority of the content is being created or produced there. It is connected throughout the world, so there's a huge volume of things that are critical to our global operation. According to both our internal standards and our JLR counterparts, it is our best-performing office.

But even when you are doing everything right in this area, you inevitably have to deal with the other side of the coin: firing members of your staff. This is the saddest moment because it means the selection and immersion process you or your team went through failed. I still remember my founding partner, Alastair Duncan, who said after a few months when we were dealing with the first problems in the behavioral space, "We are becoming a 'normal' mid-size company. If you are more than twenty people in one place, the 'normal' challenges come your way too: severe illnesses, harassments, absences, inequality issues, mismanagement, and what have you."

He was right; over the years we experienced all of these and many more challenges that you cannot even imagine. For any discussion with anyone involved, our value system had been very valuable because it served as the North Star reference for all these conversations. Every now and then such conversations involve lawyers and that is fine, but what is important is that the rationale for each decision is driven by values at every level.

FORGING A COMMON DIALOGUE

One of the things we quickly realized in setting out a core set of global beliefs is that a value system is in the eye of the beholder. Even a good job of communicating, "this is what *be bold* means, this is what *be brave* means, this is what *be honest* means" does not mean that you can declare victory. We needed to take it a step further to understand the cultural context in which this would live. Cultural vantage points and norms would have a significant role to play in how *be bold, be brave, and be honest* would be interpreted in various parts of our system. It was vital to us that everyone in the company shared the same definition of what it meant to be bold, brave, and honest.

The best starting point to achieve this was a remarkable meeting that we undertook in Paris in 2012. We brought together the entire London and Frankfurt offices. Everybody boarded a train—we were mindful to manage our costs diligently. I had asked everyone from one office to pair with someone from the other office. They had one simple task to fulfil: introduce the other person to the entire room. It did wonders. The next moment the London colleagues were people with a face and a voice who had a job to do—and vice versa. Within one afternoon, members of our UK and German local teams forged together a common understanding. Ahsan Khalon and I started the day after these special introductions with a wonderful presentation titled *What the British Say and What the British Mean*, and we got people from both teams to work out the subtle nuances and make sure people understood. That was a huge success because it allowed people to connect, and that connection started to become real; so that was the first opportunity for the values to blossom and take on life rather than being just paper on a wall or words on a piece of paper.

We had an extraordinary and surprisingly frank discussion with the UK office. The UK is probably among the politest countries in the world, but that politeness can sometimes get in the way of giving somebody the honest view on something. My personal "aha" moment shattered my assumption because of language; it's easy for the US and the UK (and other English-speaking countries, for that matter) to understand each other. However, the opposite was true, and we figured out that there was much more commonality between the Americans and the Germans in terms of their "let's get to the facts," "what's the situation" directness, which other cultures might find abrupt. The result was extraordinary, and I must say a further bond between our people developed as they came together in community.

This conversation extended to our other regions, with the most interesting result in China. Here we were not just dealing with cultural norms of expression, but with an institutionalized management practice dating back to its pre-capitalist roots. The legacy of hierarchy in Chinese management practice still pervades the business culture there. If the boss says, "It's white," it's white; if the boss says, "It's black," it's black, and you don't argue. We did not want that kind of behavior. We were able to get a universal understanding of what it meant to be bold and brave as well as honest with their local clients, but what we realized is that our people in an organizational environment of a still-hierarchical nature would require an enormous amount of support from us to have their backs as they made bold and brave proposals to a sometimes-recalcitrant local audience.

IN GOOD TIMES AND IN BAD

I always thought our values would serve us well as we grew, but I never thought they would come into focus quite like they did when we had to make some tough management decisions affecting our people. We founded the company office in Los Angeles largely because that's where Steve was based. Spark44 LA was a really great office, with great people and output. However, for practical reasons we had to bring the business much closer to the Jaguar Land Rover North American HQ in New Jersey, especially for strategic roles. A tough decision: Do we close the whole operation and bring it all to New York? Money matters would say yes. (I dare say that's how other organizations I am familiar with would look at it.) We decided we would not be doing right by our people to go there and simply say, "In two weeks, the office will be shut." Instead, we went there three and a half months in advance in order to give everybody the opportunity to adjust to the news and time to consider their professional life after Spark44. It was tough, but in hindsight, I believe those who were affected accepted that this was a behavior that they would not see anywhere else. Honesty can mean good news and bad news, too, but the spirit of honesty means doing the right thing by communicating any news to the best advantage of everyone involved.

The developments around the LA office were proof of the wisdom of this approach. In spring 2018 we agreed to shift the emphasis to make LA a creative lounge instead of a full-service office. That meant reducing our LA head count by half and shifting the remaining roles to New York, closer to the clients. Since the LA office was one of the founding offices, Global HR director Ali McManus and I went across the ocean to meet with Tony Hobley, who was running the US operation, to share the news with all staff. Before we arrived at the office, we met in the hotel lobby. We agreed this was a time for honesty and, come what may, for bravery. The pressure from our partner was not light. But we agreed we would arrive at a solution that was right for the business while respectful of everyone involved, no matter what pressures we experienced. I remember Tony saying, "Everybody's watching. We'll be remembered for how we handled this. The pressure will pass . . . a bad solution won't." In our hearts, closing, or at least downsizing, the LA office did not feel like we were doing justice to the people who had been a lighthouse for us over the years. We went into the meeting with heavy hearts.

Unfortunately, only ten months later we had to completely relocate this office to the East Coast. It was time to go back to LA and convey the bad news; we needed to close the office and bring the relevant creative positions to New York. That was something I could not delegate. But Brian Fraser, our chief creative officer, who had by now been with us for three and a half years and had fully internalized our set of values, was determined to be with me in front of all staff when the bad news had to be delivered. This is what one needs to do: celebrate the successes but also take full responsibility for the opposite.

BRAVERY IN FAIRNESS

I was determined we would not follow usual patterns in these circumstances. First, a relocation for those who wished to go to New York, ample severances for those who could not, and a final and controversial decision that we would keep the office open for specialized skills built around people we cherished. We held out until many were able to find new jobs. For us, this was the fair and proper decision. Werner's words that "values cost money" were being lived out. Our approach, consistent with our beliefs, was costing much more than adhering to what the law required. It was simply a question of what our beliefs required.

In the end, four folks came to New York, several found great jobs immediately—a good result all around. But what was really satisfying was the feedback from all other parts of the company as to how our people felt about how we dealt with it. It taught me that as leaders we are always being judged by how we live out the values we establish. Their eyes are on us . . . long may it continue.

BRING ON THE VILLAINS

So much of what we live out in concert with our values is important but unnoticed by the outside world. But that changed with the US Super Bowl in 2013, which saw the first appearance for the Jaguar brand of a host of "villains" driving Jaguars extolling their "villainous virtues": the now-award-winning and famous campaign featuring famous Hollywood British villains like Ben Kingsley, Tom Hiddleston, and Mark Strong. What I remember most is not only how it came about, but how being brave and bold and honest overcame the natural resistance to such a disruptive idea. The crucial task was the launch of the much-anticipated Jaguar F-TYPE Coupe. This was the moment to introduce the successor to the E-TYPE—the icon on which the brand's heritage was based. We needed to seize that moment and create a campaign to make a dent in the universe.

Sharing in bravery and no small amount of faith, JLR's North American Regional Director Andy Goss took the decision to book the first Super Bowl ad for Jaguar that the brand had ever placed. He was pressing for a "lighthouse moment" for the brand. The pressure was on. To achieve enhanced respect for Jaguar we needed to play on that stage, but we knew we really needed something that the world would talk about. In a good way . . .

Already in 2011, when we started our initial approach to a brand strategy, a similar thought in the space of "villains" was one of three routes for the brand we discovered in the debrief from the very first research project with Richard Auton, who was brought in to work with us by Alastair Duncan.

We all agreed on establishing a strategy for Jaguar to make a dent in the universe. Various teams worked on finding the solution, with a range of very good, but expected, expressions of British elegance, polish, and aristocratic overtones. Then a team in the UK with Matt Page and Piggy Lines could not stop but worked beyond all internal deadlines to bring their piece to the decision table. They thought, "We'll just give it a try," an illustration of *be brave* in action. They worked around the clock for two days and nights because they knew we had an upcoming decision-making forum scheduled. They sent their work through literally half an hour before the meeting. On the shared screen of on one of these GoToMeeting video calls, the slide went up: "It's good to be bad." Their bold interpretation of Britishness—the elegant but roguish nonconformist. All of us in the room, ten in all, looked around in silence, and in an instant, one piped up, "This is it."

A BRAVE STANCE

The forum for presenting the work to our Jaguar partner was called the Brand Council, which later became the Brand Committee. To stand true to our efficiency approach, it was imperative that most of the global work be reviewed by the Brand Committee so it could be shared across all the regions, with slight modifications. When we launched the Jaguar F-TYPE Coupe, we had recommended advertising in the biggest advertising platform in the world—the Super Bowl. We needed to go very big, especially in the US, to enhance brand awareness. I recall that in one of those meetings prior to the presentation of our idea, a Jaguar exec asked me, as Spark44's COO, what my role was in this process. "Well," I replied, "it is 10 percent seeing to it that we present a bold idea, and 90 percent is convincing you it is right and protecting it from attack until it is produced." Wry smiles all around. The decision we then took was unusual: "Can you please share with us three alternatives on how to do it?" Bravery emboldened us to say otherwise. We would present one idea, our *Good to Be Bad* concept, and stand behind it. No alternatives. We'd used our precious preparation time to put a bit more flesh to the bone and see how that would go and make it work and say, "Well this is it. It's this or nothing." That's the way it was presented. We partnered with Mindshare, our global media agency at the time, and we shared how creative ideas and media ideas could be equally balanced and integrated. Because we had prepared so well, there were no debates from the clients. It was a home run.

The moment you get to work that is polarizing, it gets difficult managing that piece of work through a group of many stakeholders. For any global campaign, obviously you've got central teams, you've got local teams on the client side, and you've got senior management because it has a significant impact on perception, so you have to deal with lots of people. Lots of people always have different starting points of how they measure things or how they look at work. Getting approval from a host of stakeholders would be no easy feat.

As with all full-impact advertising there was a polarizing element to this work, too. While "#GOOD TO BE BAD" was liked at the meeting room table, there were several people who called it a risk to the reputation of the brand; some clients were afraid of blowback. Our key marketing communications client, Ian Armstrong, a recognized expert in the industry and member of many industry bodies and jury boards, stood firmly behind it. He was convinced that this would take the brand to the next level despite many colleagues who were worried. I remember one saying, "Yeah, it makes sense, but for goodness' sake we don't want to be the badass car brand." We said, "Well, that's not how communication works. You're not going to be the badass car brand; you're going to be the cool car brand." At the press conference when Jaguar's first-ever Super Bowl participation was called out, the line was presented in public—a good ten weeks before the Super Bowl event. It was revealed on purpose—to learn from social listening what the impact on the brand's perception was. Guess what? Hardly any mention of "badass car brand." Jaguar's brand director at the time, Adrian Hallmark, confirmed the go-ahead for the production. Oscar-winning director Tom Hooper worked with our creative team under Werner's leadership and delivered the most effective suite of work the brand had seen in a long time. We were lucky that our team in Los Angeles was firing on all cylinders under the leadership of the office MD Milind Raval and created a communications program that was second to none. Every single customer touchpoint of the program was literally architected on a large "wall scroll" where each creative/media idea was connected to the next, with specific calls to action and key performance indicators (KPIs) illustrated. We wanted to make sure there was a purpose for every deliverable. The impact exceeded everybody's expectations.

THE RESULT

The Super Bowl appearance and subsequent campaign quickly catapulted the Jaguar brand to the tops of the minds of luxury car buyers in the US and beyond. Recognition and dialogue around villains skyrocketed, with tracking scores showing quantum increases in favorable attitudes toward the brand. To cap it off, the prestigious Effie Award for marketing effectiveness, the marketing industry's most coveted prize, awarded us the silver Effie in North America. A few months later we were awarded the bronze Global Effie as the work had been successful the world over. It was the first Global Effie for an automotive brand in ten years.

We were convinced it would do the job, and it did. For Andy Goss this campaign was the key foundation for some other work that gave momentum to Jaguar, driving sales growth over the next two years. The campaign had internal effects, too. I still remember a product presentation four years later—in 2017—about battery electric vehicles (BEVs), entitled "It's Good to be BEV."

That's how it happened, and I remember meeting one guy, David Steele, in the halls of JLR's Whitley headquarters, once the campaign broke. We hadn't been working for Land Rover at the time, and I said, "David, you know Land Rover so well, has anything on Land Rover ever gotten that kind of attraction or that kind of engagement, involvement, attention?" He said, "I've never seen anything like this."

Checking the List	
✓	What will be the source of your value system?
✓	Can you articulate your values in five words or fewer?
✓	Is your value system distinct and ownable to you?
✓	What is your plan for communicating and embedding your beliefs?
✓	How will you hold your organization accountable for them?

CHAPTER 3

A PLACE AT THE TABLE

HOW TO BUILD AN INTERDEPENDENT SKILLS AND PERSONALITY-BASED MANAGEMENT TEAM

"If he's wrong, we're going to tell him he's wrong."

"And you be sure the reverse is true. It's as simple as that. There's nothing more to it."

Letting go is key to the expansion of your enterprise. Without an alternative frame of reference, many entrepreneurs and chief executive officers at growing companies look to larger corporations for their inspiration and modeling for how they create their leadership teams, both in terms of structure and how they function. I think that's probably the last place one should look. Many organizations are still organized according to the postwar, command-and-control hierarchical structure, the type of organization codified in William H. Whyte's infamous *The Organization Man* back in 1956. The top-down, highly structured and relatively insulated organizational design of that era is ill-equipped for the kind of collaborative, rapidly moving, market-sensitive organizational design required for the twenty-first century.

For us at Spark44, we were lucky, in a way that we didn't inherit a fully painted picture with every brushstroke and color in place. Rather, we started with a blank canvas on which we could splash vivid colors and paint our future with our own broad strokes. We asked ourselves how a twenty-first-century organization behaves and how we create a management principle that allows us to be smart, flexible, and, most importantly, fast to the marketplace. Your starting point of course is the founding partners, or key employees. They are your management team. Very quickly, once the company grows, you get to a place where there are more people needed, and more leadership than just the founding partners. As we were growing quickly, the whole leadership team mushroomed, starting with founding partners, the ones who were representing the leadership of the first three offices—London, Los Angeles, and Frankfurt—as well as the two creative directors and then the leadership of our newest agency in Shanghai. Soon the various specialties such as strategic planning, retail function, and information technology functions emerged, and our leadership team was starting to look like the cast of a Hollywood epic. The question was, who was going to have a seat at the table? While we kept it loose at the beginning, it became clear as the organization was growing that it needed some sort of a logic to make it work.

INTERDEPENDENCE

One of my early bosses in the old days of McCann had a droll but accurate description of how we led the company internationally. Our conversation went like this:

"Think of us as the Roman Empire."

"What do you mean?"

"We make the advertising decisions at the center, then we tell them all to do it."

"What happens if the office doesn't want to do it?"

"Oh, they'll comply . . . like Roman times, it may take us three months to get there, but we'll burn their village down when we do."

This rather colorful picture was ever-present in my mind as I witnessed the effects of this kind of top-down thinking, how inflexible it was, how little it did to promote creativity and innovation, and how it had a wholesale inability to tap talent collaboratively. Spark44, however, focused on the concept of *interdependence*.

Interdependence is creating a team that is interlocking. It is where you recognize and bring people to the table for their strengths and none of their weaknesses. Here, you build a mosaic of individual talents all in commitment to each other, so that people are free and confident to lend their strengths, happy to have another give theirs and not look over their shoulders concerning themselves with turf. In this setup, there is no turf... or the corrosive politics that come with it. It rests entirely on collaboration. Interdependent organizational structures have enormous implications for who you select to be part of a management team. Of course, how they behave and relate to one another also affects your own role as the chief executive. You can see how our overemphasis on culture was so important because, by definition, when you are recruiting for this kind of structure, two dimensions are vital: a person's ability to fill the "technical" role required by the job, and a personality that is generous in spirit and emotionally intelligent.

THE EMOTIONALLY INTELLIGENT LEADER

With the old-fashioned, top-down command-and-control system, the CEO is effectively a commander. The leader, like any good military person, prepares orders, communicates them, and relies upon a sequencing of downward communication to ensure that the orders are carried out to the letter by each and every person in the organization all the way down to the lowly private. An interdependent organization requires a different management philosophy. It means that you go from being commander to being coach. Arguably, the most important skillset that you need to have, and the one that any entrepreneur needs to grow and develop, is the ability to connect with people and encourage them. It is vital to connect the members of your team to ensure that they maintain their interdependence. Think of your title as the chief encouragement and facilitation officer. This means you're spending your time with each team member individually, and with them as an operating whole, reaffirming the overarching goals of the organization while also imparting all important elements of the organization's value system—which in our case is *be bold, be brave, and be honest.* Put another way: you're Luke Skywalker, Obi Wan, and Yoda all rolled into one.

A CLASH OF TITANS

Sometimes, the things you institutionalize materialize in ways you never expected. I remember bringing a new executive to the organization, a fine account leader named Jonathan Hill. As part of his immersion in and orientation to the company, I thought it would be good for him to sit in on routine conversations so he could absorb things, especially how we dealt with each other. It happened that we were in Los Angeles visiting Tony Hobley, the managing director of our office there. Tony and I had scheduled a GoToMeeting with Steve to talk about a US-specific program. Within seconds of our sitting down together, Steve launched a firm and unvarnished criticism of some of our recent decisions, respectful of course, but mincing no words. In no uncertain terms, I made it clear to him that he was very much alone with his view. Jonathan, in typical British style, kept his reserve. After we parted, Jonathan, looking incredulous, asked Tony, "My word, does Ralf always speak with him that way?" Tony said to Jonathan, "Only when he needs real clarity—now you know why I call him 'Fearless Ralf.'" I said: "If he's wrong, we're going to tell him he's wrong. And you be sure the reverse is true. It's as simple as that. There's nothing more to it."

I made sure we established a climate where people were free to express themselves without hesitation; there would be no elephants in the rooms for us. But make no mistake: this situation, while involving only the four of us, became known in many parts of the organization—and we wanted it to be that way as it had been our intention to create an environment without fear.

A defining event happened, again in a completely unplanned fashion, which is still talked about and in some ways defines how our interdependent leadership team operates. This was our third big Finca Meeting. Gonzalo Ocio, our managing director in Spain, secured us this great place near Madrid called Pedraza. So, on the opening day, Steve stands in front of the screen and talks about something, and I'm at the other end of the room. In between us, there are sixty people. Steve makes a point, and I don't agree with the point. I mean, I *really* don't agree with the point. At which point I assert, rather forcefully, from the back of the room, *"Steve, it's wrong. It's not right. It's different. It's this, and then it's this. You have no clue about this. It's just wrong."* Steve replied emphatically that *I* had no idea what *I* was talking about, and just like McEnroe and Borg in the fifth set at the 1980 Wimbledon final, this went on for ten minutes. Back and forth, heads turning with every play. Now, remember, this was the first time we had had this Finca Meeting with all these people from all these new offices coming in. The majority of them knew me. Half of them didn't know Steve; it was the first time they had met him. Then, in the heat of the exchange, just as quickly as it had started, we smirked at each other and said, "Okay, we'll agree to disagree." We then walked over and hugged each other and just said to everybody in the room, "This is the way we do it."

"I remember it distinctly," Steve recalled. "Ralf and I were arguing back and forth, and I kind of picked up on everybody around the room in a state of shock so I pushed it more, because I knew they were witnessing something important, the ability for anyone in the company to express themselves with passion and to defend their point of view but also to demonstrate that we would still be friends and teammates at the end of it."

POLLINATION

As you establish your multi-office footprint, the question arises, how do you connect with both the leadership of these offices and the people across the world? What's your role? You have found highly qualified people with local market expertise to run these locations, so now, what do you do? When we were reflecting on how we operated, Steve put it aptly: "We were like pollinating bees." I know this image was unlikely to be found in a management text, but it was a spirited definition of emotionally intelligent leadership—namely, the ability to connect with the emotional motives of your team, being aware of your own, and shaping positive actions as a result. Neither presiding, nor controlling, but floating across the team offering wisdom, insight, and guidance, maintaining clarity of vision, keeping people connected and motivated, and, of course, adjudicating and sorting through conflict. And, while we're on the subject, conflict is a vital and healthy part of a well-oiled collaborative team. Old-fashioned command-and-control systems seek to winnow conflict out; as a consequence, you get compliance, not innovation. Creativity and breakthrough come from well-managed conflict of ideas and possibilities. Steve and I realized much of this would come from the "cultural permission" we gave the team in the form of our own relationship and behavior.

THE STUMP SPEECH

So, here's a handy tip. Take a page out of what political candidates do and write yourself a "stump" speech. Now, I am originally from Germany, and while I had heard that term before, I never knew what it meant. In fact, stump speeches are what early American politicians delivered when they went from town to town. They would stand up on a tree stump or other improvised stage, so as to be seen by the crowd, and deliver their speech. A "stump speech" became the phrase describing the short, standardized speech a candidate repeats verbatim to each audience on his or her visit around the country. As you write your stump speech, first collect your thoughts around the big emotive goal everyone is there to achieve, then recite your value systems, along with your series of maxims (like, "if it doesn't get measured it doesn't get done," etc.) that you want your people to remember. Then, in each encounter across the globe, be sure you are delivering all or part of these themes.

Remember, people forget easily, and it is up to you to be the cultural glue that holds your people together. Think of the image of a pebble dropping in a still pond. The little concentric circles emanate from the center outward. That's what you are doing. As you connect with your network, you will inspire them in turn to share these things with others.

It is like you're lighting a flame. Insist on a conversation by video instead of one by phone, if you can't be there in person; let them see you live. Make videos and distribute them regularly. People love them, because, remember, they have signed up for you.

VIRTUAL WERNER

There really is no substitute for physical presence. I would encourage any leader of a multi-location or multinational organization to have a presence in as many of her or his locations, especially the key ones, as is humanly possible. You really can't overestimate how much equity there is in your presence, or how inspiring and memorable it is to be close to the people who make up your organization. Of course, with all the demands on your time it isn't always possible to do so, and you can use technology to your advantage with as many video conference meetings with your people as you can handle. We did find in fact find another way, one that began as a joke but actually became one of Spark44's most memorable and iconic forms of presence. We called it *Virtual Werner.*

Werner Krainz was one of the founding partners of Spark44, a fine man and a brilliant creative director who spent tireless hours traversing our network inspiring creative people to create the best work of their lives. But even Werner was not able to be in more than one place at a time. So, we leveraged technology in an unprecedented way. We invested in a Segway with an iPad mounted on top of it for the Los Angeles office. Werner could move the Segway remotely from London, allowing him, with a FaceTime connection, to talk directly with teams 6,000 miles away. People just loved it. At any given point virtual

Werner could be heard around the network speaking about the inspirations of creative greatness and how his team needed to swing for the fences on behalf of our client Jaguar Land Rover as well as our own fortunes, to be famous for the work we're doing. Imagine having the opportunity to speak to offices around the world in an engaging fashion without having the need to be there in person. Very soon people began to modify versions of Virtual Werner: at any given point he might be wearing a beard or a beret. At one point, rumor has it, he was in a miniskirt . . . but don't quote me on that.

FUNCTIONAL LEADS

There is a unique way to organize your interdependent management team. The first, obviously, is on the basis of their individual functional area. That is where most organizations begin and end. The second dimension, and the magic, is to give each of them additional portfolios that are global in nature. We called them *voices*. They had a responsibility for an initiative that went beyond the functional. This concept of *voices* provides organizational clarity on ultimate responsibility for each initiative but, more importantly, "it" provides a voice and a place at the table for a vitally important company initiative. This approach allows subject matter and teamwork to build horizontally across your management team and thereby across your entire organization. This means no one has blinders on. When you have a diverse set of leadership members, they all have their strengths, and one of your roles as a global leader is to make those strengths available to the entire organization and think about how you can leverage them in the best possible way. Georg Mankel, our retail expert, quickly became the go-to person for all questions anyone in any of our offices had when it came to developing cut-through ideas that showed an impact at the retail level. While his expertise was leveraged for external client projects, there were other areas of expertise that had a tremendous impact internally. Emma, for instance, is probably one of the best people in managing complex projects and complex processes which, obviously, was one of the reasons we hired her for the Birmingham operation. When she was able to complete her initial task of making sure that agency in Birmingham was a well-oiled-machine, we asked her to take on a lead role as global head of operations in order to make sure that the same operational standards applied across all offices. Once Emma had established everything that needed to be established in the Birmingham office, she had the capacity to do it globally. In 2018 we introduced SparkShare, which was our name for the project management tool that enables us to have a view of who's doing what where in what timeframe. It was a smash hit everywhere.

VOICES

The concept of functional leads had started when we laid out our foundational structure. Creating an organizational design that did not allow for siloes to establish themselves was paramount. Steve, Werner, Alastair, Bruce, Alistair, and I had seen this in all organizations where we had worked before. It killed innovative ideas, often got them not even presented to the clients because these ideas had originated in the "wrong silo." So, we established the idea of the four voices (by the way, this is one of the two 4s in 44—the other 4 stood for the 4 founding offices). The account guy was responsible for representing the voice of the client. That was key. You must always be sure the voice of the customer is heard. In turn, creative was the voice of the agency; creativity in all forms is as essential as the product the agency produces. Retail was the voice of the trade—especially when you operate in the automotive sector it is critical, as retailers are critical for the implementation of fully integrated communication programs as the end-customers are legally their customers. And strategic planning was the voice of the consumer—understanding the behaviors and insights that trigger actions. Ensuring all voices make themselves heard is critical.

Now, there's natural friction in all of this. You never want that to go away. You want each of your voices to speak with passion on behalf of the area that they have a responsibility for. Your role is to facilitate and, of course, adjudicate between each of these competing voices. Most importantly to ensure that they are all recognized and value each other as integral parts.

EXCHANGE PROGRAMS

Bringing cohesion to networks involves any and all means to connect people on an emotional level. We created an innovative program, on a local level, to send our best and brightest young people to other offices in the system for short durations. This was a simple program with multidimensional benefits. First, it was a wonderful motivator and reward system for bright up-and-coming people. Second, it was an opportunity to bring needed resources into offices where there was a spike in activity but a shortage of talent. Most importantly, it was a means by which people could come to know each other by working together and thereby increasing the bond and strength of relationships that would continue once these individuals returned to their home offices. Two of our local managing directors, Gonzalo Ocio in Spain and Leticia Thenard in Brazil, created SparkBnB, which involved sending people over for a month or two to swap jobs and apartments with each other. That helped both of them individually, and it helped both offices.

GIVE HER MY TICKET

There were two key characteristics that we were looking to address when we were building our international management team: generosity of spirit and collaboration. Collaboration is born from a culture of generosity, one that I saw sorely lacking in the command-and-control structures that I experienced earlier in my career. Siloed, top-down structures separate, and in the separation, whether by conscious act or not, competition inevitably surfaces. Now I do believe in healthy competition, but left unchecked as it is in many organizations, competitive cultures can morph into predatory ones, where individual units compete for income and resources. As a consequence, collaboration in those contexts is anathema and literally impossible.

Command-and-control structures create hierarchy and communicate that some people in the organization are more or less important than others. Flat organizations communicate that power is widely distributed across the organization and that there is importance placed on every individual in the organization. This approach is in fact a testament to the strength of the culture that you have built. What was always critical to us was that no matter who it was individually or what their hierarchical status was, the only thing that mattered was the individual themselves and their contribution.

There is probably no better testimony to this than a gesture by one of our people that, as I reflect back on my McCann Erickson days, would have been impossible and perceived by the participants to be career suicide. Bringing the Land Rover business into Spark44 was a massive job for many. But some of us were obviously in the eye of the storm, managing the transition of more than sixty relationships that existed previously with different agency partners across the world into Spark44. I wanted to thank them with a memorable experience. The upcoming Wimbledon Grand Slam tennis championships, of which Jaguar was a proud sponsor, was the perfect opportunity. We invited the key people and they were treated like VIPs. In many ways it was better than a bonus, because these tickets were virtually impossible to obtain. We held a little ceremony and over a glass of champagne awarded the six team members the tickets with a statement of appreciation. During the cocktail event that followed, Kate Moore, one of the six key people approached me and said, "Listen, I appreciate and thank you very much for the recognition, but actually there's a young woman in the London team, Maria Samartian. She is the one who should go. She gave so much of herself." Maria, at the time, was an office assistant, but she was doing such an outstanding job that she later became the assistant of the MD; everybody in the office valued her contribution. Kate said, "You know what? Give her my ticket. She's worth it." On that day, it was really fun watching the dynamics.

The five people showed up and whom should they see but Maria, who had taken Kate's place. They were taken aback at first, but as I recount, They all realized in an instant why she was there and congratulated her profusely. In that moment, and in that gesture, there was the evidence of everything Steve and I set out to build.

THE AMBASSADOR

I'm going to go back to a starting premise, and that is, entrepreneurs by definition are idea people, people who are visionaries, but . . . they reach a point in the growth of their business where they have to change. They have to do something differently than they did before. I like to use the analogy that you're on a journey with baggage, and there's some baggage you have to take with you because it is essential. Then, there's stuff you need to leave home. You don't need it and don't want it. Then you have to take some new stuff with you. As a creator of an organization, it is vital that you take with you the value systems and cultural underpinnings that define your organization. As you expand across locations and operating competencies, you must leave behind any notion that you have the ability to manage these things yourself or have more than a working knowledge of what many areas of your company are actually doing. What you need to take with you is the ability to establish your presence and influence, your standards, expectations, and beliefs so that all of the people in your organization, however far they might be from you physically, feel them in the same way equally around the world.

Through time, as your organization grows, your role shifts as you become more ambassador than boss. You have to put in place bosses, and they have to put in place bosses, and that's the only way it grows. You have to take your hands off the wheel. Let the people you have empowered do it, let them make their experiences—but always be available for advice. Entrepreneurship is a highly emotional journey. In so many ways this new phase presents a different kind of challenge. It's like changing your lifestyle, going from being the boss of something where you're hands-on, as many entrepreneurs are; they're in it, and they're loving the fight. Now you're finding yourself in the role of ambassador. It will be hard. It's kind of like watching your kids grow up and leave the house. If you've put the right people in place then you must let them fly.

For you, it's learning to derive an entirely new form of satisfaction out of what you create. In the early stages, satisfaction came from that which you created, the intrinsic product or service that you innovated and how you brought it to the marketplace. In this new phase of your career, satisfaction is drawn from observing and supporting others to be the best they can be and seeing them create in the same way that you did and make their mark on the organization and the world at large. If you let yourself go, there is no greater satisfaction than this. If you put the right people in place and you've seen results, then you have to trust that it's working. If you put what you think are the right people in place and there are no results, then you've got to change the people. In our situation, I felt it was the right people. The results were definitely there, so hands off. I could trust them. Now, I had to force myself to allow them to take my hands off the operational details, and it wasn't easy. You, as the founder, have to allow people to come at you and tell you, "Back off. I got it."

Checking the List

✓	Do you know who will make up your evolved leadership team?
✓	Is this team diverse?
✓	Will they be able to challenge you?
✓	Do you have a core message for them and for the firm at large?
✓	Do you have an employee feedback mechanism?

CHAPTER 4

TALENT CENTRICITY

TWENTY-FIRST CENTURY HUMAN RESOURCES

"Well, you know what, this really feels like day one."

"You've got exactly the same spirit, the same desire to break with convention. Keep going!"

Throughout my advertising career one of the things that always amazed me was how little attention was paid to employee development. Whether it was orientation for new employees or training and development evaluation for providing critical feedback, my view is that the advertising industry was far behind other industry counterparts. When we sat down to create Spark44, we started with how we felt about the organization we wanted to build. The first order of business upon the founding of the company would be our approach to the talent management process, which would remain central to the attentions of the senior management team. I pledged to avoid the trap that many corporations fall into, focusing on the finances and operations. Rather, I made my job first and foremost about focusing on talent, because it was our view that if you get the talent right, the money follows. There were several specific initiatives of which I am immensely proud. For our Accelerator initiative in particular, our company was identified by an outside organization as being one of the few that actually achieved its goals. The ability to create virtual working groups globally and to make them work successfully was something they had not seen at that level of intensity before. I encapsulated our task in three elements: mining, motivating, and measuring.

MINING

We as founding partners often talked of building a pirate ship—the opposite of the "navy." All of us had a history with the "navy"—the big advertising holding companies. Now we got together on this vessel filled with people who came to embark on a decidedly different voyage and who were prepared to sail against the current of conventional wisdom. Finding these people would be no easy task. A business like ours is only creating value if the talent that is in the business provides it. There are no machines, no factories. There's only human capital, and in our early days we had a pretty clear view of what we were supposed to be doing, in terms of the capabilities we needed. The real question was what culture we were prepared to build and what talent we would bring in. As you may recall, each of the founders was in different region of the world, and each of us took a slightly different approach to finding our pirates. Some of us looked into our Rolodex and our little books with all the names and built the team around people that we already knew. I decided not to do that. From my perspective, finding new and different people required a new and different approach. I still remember we didn't have an office; we didn't yet have a company. Yet we were trying to convince people that this would be the place they should come to. I made prodigious use of various social media channels to identify talent by capabilities because we had to build a very international setup based in Frankfurt. Apart from specialized communications competencies, we needed people who were fluent in Italian, French, Spanish, and Russian.

MINING MARATHON

It took quite some time to identify potential candidates. I then invited all of them into a coffee shop, one after the other, for their job interviews. I set myself up in the corner of the place with literally a back-to-back flow from seven-thirty in the morning to eight o'clock at night. For pure scheduling reasons, it turned out that only female candidates were being interviewed on the first day. I will probably not forget the owner of that coffee shop who sheepishly came up to me saying, "Well, welcome to our shop; we haven't met yet, but you've become a very frequent guest." I think it was day two, actually. "We're all wondering, what the hell are you doing? There's all these young women that are coming to see you and you're chatting with them and then they leave and the next one comes." I said, "Yeah, relax, man, relax. It's all good. That's going to continue for a while." Little did he know he was witness to my determination to go against industry standards and ensure a rightful place at our firm for highly qualified people leveraging the positive impact of diversity, at all levels of our company. What became clear was candidates that fell into two categories. There was one group of people that thought, "Well, this is interesting. Can I have a job description?" And there was another group of people that said, "Well, this is very interesting. I want to be part of building something." For the ones who asked for a job description, my standard response was, "Well, we don't have one, but we're happy for you to write it once you've started! Your job description is a white sheet of paper and you're invited to build it with us." Very quickly, quite a number of those people made it clear that they did not want to do this. I really think they thought I was crazy.

It was obvious that these weren't the right people. They might have had the right skills but would never prosper in the controlled chaos of what Spark44 would become. Their attitude wasn't the one that you need when you want to expand your startup. To this day, I remind myself of that, and I remind everybody that when we're hiring people, we're looking for a mindset of wanting to build and create something and not merely looking for people to fill a job. This is a crucial moment, because often during the early days of innovation and creativity startup owners believe they need to become institutionalized. It's the kiss of death.

MOTIVATING

Bringing new people to an organization is such an important process. Yet, when I look back on my career, I witnessed the insane process that most advertising agencies engaged in: hiring people, throwing them in the deep end of the pool, and abandoning them to their own devices. Countless people failed to succeed in these crazy circumstances. For us, acculturation to the value system of Spark44, developing an interdependency with existing team members very quickly, was, in my view job number one. The orientation process at Spark44 was a carefully choreographed affair. From my perspective it was one of the best investments we made in time and energy. The first task was to organize in-depth sessions with key members of our management team but also to have them visit at least two members of our team in other markets. The purpose: to learn our value systems directly from the people living them.

In early 2019 we had an exchange of the leaders in key hub offices in Shanghai, in Frankfurt, and in New York within six months. All of them had earned their stripes in the "navy." Now they were embarking on a different course, which required them to *unlearn* some of the traits they had grown up with in their past. Our extended hub structure allowed the leaders of the smaller offices to help and support the cultural immersion—permanent reminders when "navy behavior" seemed to be overriding what we expected in our culture and from our value system of *be bold, be brave, be honest*. Quite a journey for all, but a great testimony to a culture that had embedded itself and did not require the CEO to step in.

THE TOOLS OF THE TRADE

I know that when one mentions a process or tool, the words mundane and rigid often come to mind. Well, that depends entirely on what the tool or the process is. I felt it was vitally important to establish a means by which we could both motivate and measure our people, providing them with a constant source of feedback and the guidance to grow in their jobs. We decided to introduce a quarterly process of evaluations. We would dedicate ourselves to a process of two-way feedback for each and every person in the organization, including myself. This ran counter to the total absence of evaluations in many places, but conducting evaluations frequently through the year provided a pathway for the growth of our people. Initially the evaluations were designed around individual competencies, like creativity or strategy. We quickly figured out that we would do ourselves a big favor if we didn't separate the evaluations by profession or by capability, but actually connected them with the values that we wanted the business to represent. In constructing this program, it became all too clear to me why programs of this kind are not implemented. It takes an enormous amount of time and energy. Imagine doing this with about twenty people, half an hour each, meaning ten hours in a quarter. That's a day, or more likely two days, with preparation and with follow-ups. Multiply this by four times a year and you get quite a commitment. We were convinced, however, that this, rather than managing granularity, was the true role of management, so we committed to exploring a quarterly program

We linked the evaluative criteria to *be bold, be brave, and be honest*, with ten specific evaluative criteria in each category. We measured everybody against those on a scale from 1 to 5. It was a rolling process, with the current quarter's evaluation becoming the basis for the next quarter's evaluations. We built a "stop-continue-start" logic of counseling:

STOP: That's not so great; why don't you stop doing that?

CONTINUE: Continue doing that. That's great!

START: Hey, why don't you start doing that?

The program went through the entire agency, from new hires to the CEO. Everybody was evaluated. The effect was utterly transformative. Rather than a punitive, "putting people on the griddle" type of affair, it became a pep rally, providing people with rolling motivational feedback to help them become greater than they believed they were. We let them know how brilliant they were but also how much more effective they could be.

Evaluations must be meaningful and relate to compensation. We linked the process to a bonus, which actually was a percentage of a week's salary, that was paid out every quarter. It wasn't big money, but it was still something that you could, at whatever level, celebrate and just have a bit more to spend that quarter. It was a mechanism to ensure that people took it seriously, because the moment money is involved, there is a different kind of energy. In the beginning, we did this with Excel spreadsheets because it was just twenty people per office. So not a big deal. As we grew, we moved into a software solution, with a company that specialized in doing online evaluations. They customized the system for us, and we've been operating with that ever since.

When we were in years six and seven, we went through evaluation discussions with a thousand-odd people, four times a year. We realized logistically it had become too much. Part of the reason people were not happy about evaluations four times a year was because the line management was spread far too wide. There were too many people reporting to some leaders, which meant doing evaluations four times a year was not like one and a half or two days. It was like a full week. We looked at that and said, "Well, then let's not cure the symptom; let's cure the cause."

There was a group of people who said, "Well, let's move to twice a year." I was not happy about the twice a year because six months is too long, and you don't really remember what you talked about six months ago when you talk to so many people. Eventually, we moved to three times a year, but we also took the opportunity to straighten up the organizational hierarchy so that line managers would be able to spend time with everyone individually.

That wasn't the objective of the thing, but it became clear that it was the smart and efficient thing to do. When we moved from four to three, we also thought it was time to find a name for the thing because our internal term for it was "the quarterly evaluation." Not an inspiring initiative, but a bureaucratic task. We said, "Well, let's do something different."

THE LARRYS

There was a wonderful guy in our Toronto office by the name of Larry Uniac. He was a producer, a respected veteran in an office where he was surrounded by twenty somethings. He was the elder statesman in that office and there was no question he loved his role. The young staff adored him. Beyond the Toronto office, Larry was well-respected by everybody, known far and wide as someone to call, who would never say no, and who could always be counted on to pitch in. One dark day in 2018, we received the news that Larry had been diagnosed with stage 4 cancer. Our dear Larry was dying. Now it happened that Larry loved the evaluation process; he was a strong ambassador for these performance evaluations, referring to them as "possibility" sessions. He saw them not as a punitive or rote progress, but as a people-centered "experience." Larry had always said, "The one thing I like about Spark44 is that there are these quarterly evaluations and we really take our people seriously. We take time and interest to look at them carefully, hear them out, and we listen to them. Then we agree on what we're doing together, see what's possible, gear each other for it, and let them fly!"

We lost Larry all too soon after he delivered the terrible news of his illness. His loss struck our Toronto team and beyond profoundly. None of us was quite sure how to mark this sad event—until we toasted Larry at a dinner in London with our leadership team. The team had debated during the afternoon how to improve the performance evaluation process for our people. To mark the changes, we decided it needed a new identity. I was sitting at the dinner table over a glass of wine when Ali McManus, our global HR Director "Well, why don't we call the evaluations from now on the *Larrys*?" It was unanimous in an instant. Polarities would stand for the power of human energy, a possibility, generosity of spirit, everything that Larry embodied. We made quite a fanfare not only to remember our dear Larry, but to announce the Larrys to our worldwide organization. Larry will always be with us. His wife and family were profoundly touched and really appreciated that we took that decision, a true sentiment of what we believe and how Larry embodied it so fully.

THE STAFF SURVEY

When the company tripled in size during 2015, we upgraded our HR capabilities and ways of working. It was important. Gone were the days when the founders knew every staff member. It became virtually impossible to understand how our people felt about the organization. Information got filtered through management layers, which was not what we had envisaged when we started Spark44. It was important that we still listened to our staff's voices. So, Ali McManus introduced SPARKLIFE—an online staff survey which allowed all of our associates to participate in giving feedback. And they did.

The evaluation system was based on a scoring system from 1 to 5, with 5 being the best. There were a host of offices that were always in the 4 range with, most between 3.5 and 4. Three was the median. Sometimes, it showed the obvious—but when you see it in black on white it is something fundamentally different than having your—or your peers'—gut suggest that there was something not the way it was supposed to be. It was a perfect temperature check, revealing which managers were able to convey our values to our people. Some of our larger offices struggled; the growth curve had been too steep, and the figures and percentages showed the results clearly: a huge number of employees who heard all the great stories of our inception but did not feel the "heart of Spark44" in their everyday jobs.

For me, this tool became a hugely important seismograph of how our organization was performing, next to our work output or our financial performance. Without such a thing, it is very difficult to grasp what is really going on if your organization has become much larger in a short period of time. It triggered key decisions about leadership changes—the numbers just don't lie.

THE EVALUATION TRYPTIC

It is likely that many of you have evaluation programs of varying kinds. So, here's an opportunity for you to up your game and connect your employee "health" with the health of your business and that of your client relationships. We began with a simple hypothesis: employee health is directly correlated with client satisfaction and office-by-office financial results. Customarily we looked at these independently; however, evaluating them in an interconnected way, we thought, might reveal powerful conclusions and a powerful business-management tool. We were soon proven right.

The SPARKLIFE survey was one component, the Larry scores average aggregated by office another. Once we had enough tracking data after a few years, we overlaid the two. In addition, we also had a client/agency survey; in 2019, with robust data, we ran correlations of all three. And here we were: client and staff satisfaction showed a high correlation; "happy staff" equaled "happy clients." No surprise. But when we looked at another correlation, we were shocked. The offices that had the highest average Larry scores showed the highest level of client dissatisfaction. Something wasn't right.

Why? Because managers had given Larry scores as a favor or compensation for other issues. The real purpose—to give an accurate view on our associates' performance—had become a second thought. The number one thought became "make your staff happy with money." Once we had that data, the numbers confirmed our decisions on some significant management changes; we wanted to make sure that performance benefited our clients and our people.

INCLUSION

As I reflect on the community of people we built at Spark44, I note with pride that we are made up of forty-eight nationalities working in nineteen offices, a company that broke every industry standard from a diversity point of view, with 50 percent women in our workforce and diverse representation at the operating committee level. That diversity was also visible in relation to ethnicity across significant positions: statistics published by the various advertising industry bodies in key markets showed that Spark44 was way ahead of industry averages. I get calls from industry leadership asking me how we did it. Did you do that via quota? How did you get to that? Agencies are terrible with this, and you succeeded. What was the magic?

I will confess here that when I got asked by a journalist for the first time in 2016, "What's your gender split?" I didn't know, and we had reached above a thousand employees. Promising to research this, I asked our HR team to figure it out. When they came back with the numbers, we were taken aback: our 1,050 people at the time included 526 women and 524 men. I didn't believe it. I said, "Can you check the numbers? That's too good to be true because whenever you look at that anywhere else, it's like 70-30, 80-20, 60-40, maximum. They went back, checked the numbers, and the numbers stayed the way they were. It was and still is an industry-shattering result. The question is, if we were not hiring by quota, how did this happen?

I believe strongly that you don't structure or hire for diversity, you structure and hire for inclusion. Do that and it all takes care of itself. We didn't recruit in the conventional way, looking for a qualification to match a narrow job description. We chose people who grasped our vision and who would write their own contribution. This inevitably led to a wide array of people. I'm confident that if we hired specifically to match job descriptions we would've ended up with the usual result. That said, we would love to have more women in our leadership team. But sometimes it is really tough; we were hiring for our new leadership in the US and made it very clear to the talent search company that we were supportive of a balanced gender approach. The longlist arrived: 38 male, 2 female. A similar situation happened just a few weeks later in the UK, which reduced the hiring managers to despair—where would we find that candidate to succeed in our approach for a diverse team structure? The senior leadership team is currently two-thirds male, one-third female. The good news is, if you look at the office MDs, it's 50-50 male and female. Certain departments have a higher female than male presence, some the opposite. But, overall, I think we can proudly say that it doesn't matter whether you're male or female, it's about what you bring to the table.

We're glad of the great people in our teams, no matter where they operate—and of achieving such a diverse workforce. This is the one thing of which I am most satisfied.

FOSTERING COLLABORATION

The magic of Spark44 is its ability to collaborate. Our organization is, by definition, one that behaves in a borderless fashion. Our culture, our organization design, structure, and process are all designed to allow for shape shifting, virtual team formation, and a spirited collaboration. As we have eliminated divisional heads and specialized organization design, we lack the internal struggles for control. The centricity of the issue at hand dictates the leadership of any given team. People understand this and know that at any given point they may lead a team in a particular effort, given their specialization or will give over control to another based upon a particular client's requirement. We don't have to struggle toward it as the rest of our industry does; it is simply woven into the fabric of our culture.

It is safe to say that collaboration is an outcome based on the value system of the firm, the organization and design structure, and individual leadership, as well as office specializations. We rejected all of the old organization design idioms of our industry and the result is a seamless and ever-shifting series of virtual teams at work on behalf of our clients.

Obviously, as Spark44 was built as a company based in Los Angeles, London, Frankfurt, and Shanghai at the same time, you couldn't ignore the fact that it wasn't an American company. It wasn't an English company, wasn't a German company, wasn't a Chinese company. It was a global company. I remember we were always asked, where are your headquarters? We always said, "We don't have a headquarters, our headquarter is GoToMeeting and FaceTime and every now and then we meet wherever we are, either in London or in the States or Germany or China." This is culturally significant because by definition we are not sending a signal of what portion of the world has some kind of cultural significance or a signal as to what group of people is aligned with leadership. Everyone is.

TRAINING AND DEVELOPMENT

As the company was growing and building more capabilities, it became obvious that there was an opportunity to train people better and ensure that their capabilities and their competencies would always be at the forefront of our industry. We created a program called the Accelerators in connection with Hyper Island, the consultancy in the digital space. Our brilliant mind Ahmed Hasan defined, spearheaded, and piloted the initiative which was then implemented as a global program by Bernardo Jun, one of our most cosmopolitan thought leaders. In his view—and mine—the Spark44 business model is unique in that it has one P&L for one global client. One of the greatest advantages of this business model is that you create a group of people who increasingly get used to seeing the whole company as a single entity rather than multiple offices and fiefdoms.

It is perhaps this engrained way of seeing the company that encouraged Bernardo Jun, who ran our office in Dubai, and the Spark44 Accelerators to try something that in any other company would have been dubbed naïve. The Spark44 Accelerators is a group of people who took a "digital transformation course" together with Hyper Island, and, inspired by the many learnings, committed to be the agents of change inside the company. They presented a white paper, the "Spark44 Innovation Roadmap," in May 2018 to us executives, and just one month later the course was completed. Once it was approved, they started implementing the roadmap by planning, designing, and implementing a six-month innovation course called the "Global Innovation Tribes." This course, launched in October 2018, would group colleagues around the world in "tribes" of six to seven people, mostly people who would have never talked to each other, and have them learn, think, and work together. So, you have a group of people whom the company sends to take a course, and six months later they are implementing their own version of the course internally at a global scale. Not at a department or office level, but at a global scale!

If putting a global training program in place in barely six months could be dubbed as naïve in other companies, expecting colleagues from around the world to opt in to join the program—when the program was not from a "hotshot" institution but an internal one, when there was no "star lecturer," when everyone had been warned that they would need to commit at least four hours per week (and the list goes on)—may have been dubbed as delusional. Well, a hundred colleagues from thirteen offices around the world joined the first wave of the program, and a total of seven tribes ended up presenting their final "sprints" to the Spark44 management. The program not only taught colleagues new tools and techniques but it helped connect colleagues, reinforcing the unique Spark44 culture. And while the core objective of the program was centered on "learning" rather than "output," the tribes that reached the final presentations encouraged management to put some of these ideas in front of the global JLR clients! Not bad for a potentially naïve and delusional endeavor.

One of the ultimate goals was to see if Spark44 could evolve to be a company that did global sprints as a norm. You may not think that this is a big deal, but if you look into the literature about "creative sprints" or "design sprints," most recommend that sprints be done with the participants sharing the same space and with participants blocking entire days away from their day-to-day work. Encouraged by the results of the Global Innovation Tribes and multiple global sprints that we ran, we started to conduct global sprints on live global client briefs beginning in 2019. While we did not expect to have blockbuster ideas come up from the global sprints from day one, we believed that it was important to give it a go. First, because global sprints reinforce culture regardless of the outcome; they connect people across the world; they remove silos between offices and functions and bring younger colleagues closer to more senior ones. Second, because we have a unique business model and culture that enables global sprints and it would be a waste of "collective intelligence" not to leverage it. And, third, because the potential benefits of global sprints—truly global and integrated work from all the corners of the world for all the corners of the world—are too big not to give it a go.

By definition we were determined not to follow the classic "put people in a room for a day and then disband" methodology. It had to be more organic, to be a means by which people would not only learn things but would come together to form a more unified organization on an ongoing basis. It would be virtual, and people would not be required to join; they would opt in.

Bernardo, our multicultural genius from Spain with Korean background who worked with us in Madrid and in Singapore and was heading the Dubai office at the time, took the mantle of driving this effort. He created a structure that consisted of three pillars: *tribes, loyalty,* and *enlistment.*

Tribes

The first notion is how people would come together: never by region or office, but across borders and work specialization. The tribes were the various teams of people that were put together, bonding and forming relationships as they learned. Soon, 10 percent of the entire organization was voluntarily joining, with over twenty webinars. People were working with various tech tools; there were collaborations with various universities on certain initiatives and programs. What it really did, beyond any specific knowledge enhancement in a certain area, was to create friends among these multi-office tribes. There's no such thing as a London tribe or a Frankfurt tribe or a Sydney tribe. They are tribes with people from Frankfurt, from the US, and they're just working together.

Even as we've gone through quite a bit of restructuring with some people leaving, all those people stayed connected and built their programs and their initiatives. I am convinced that when we encountered challenges and setbacks, the power of the tribes is what helped us endure.

Loyalty

To a degree you can say it's a training program. I would actually say it's a loyalty program, because people all of a sudden can connect with other people and really do something together. It makes people loyal to one another. These were six-month programs, so people were engaged, and it's encouraging when you see it happen. These programs also brought an increased sense of shared ambition and shared pride over collective achievements.

Enlistment

One of the requirements for members of the tribes who opted into the program was to take back into their units all that they had learned and share it in a formal setting with their colleagues. In the spirit of tribes, their objective was to develop unique formations of individuals across disciplines so as to foster our continuing culture of collaboration and interdependence. They took on this mantle enthusiastically, enjoying the role of ambassador to any member of the accelerator community.

THE INFLUENCER STRATEGY

We created a program together with Neil Cassie from The Cassie Partnership, which he called the "influencer strategy." The program involved identifying key talent from various offices who were not in leadership positions to bring them to a place and give them the opportunity to help shape our future. They were brought together to answer questions such as "Where will Spark44 be in 2021?" and "How do you get there?"

We identified twelve special people, linked them to our senior leadership team, gave them the vision for the company, and said, "How would you suggest we bring this to life?" They were given eight weeks, with three physical interactions, but everything else was virtual. About halfway through, they allowed me to have a peek under the hood at their progress. It was breathtaking. My instant feedback was, "Well, you know what, this really feels like 2011. It feels like you are the ones that my colleagues and I were when we founded the company. You've got exactly the same spirit, the same desire to break with convention. Keep going!"

After eight weeks they made their presentation to the leadership committee. It was probably the single most exciting meeting I attended in my years at Spark44. I'm sure everyone in the room would agree. Not only did it provide us with new initiatives, new views, and methods to advance our company, but in a strange way it was a renewal of our vows. The commitment to our value systems and belief in the journey of creating something different was being celebrated. From recommendations of the influencers, every senior leader and office head got one goal to bring to life in the next twelve months. Every single initiative recommended was to be taken seriously and implemented. It was a huge commitment, and it became an unbreakable connection between the executive team and those influencers. In typical Spark44 fashion, it spread across the entire organization. Local offices began creating their own influencer programs. I can say the actions that have been taken will make a significant difference in the company. As of this writing there are nearly forty specific initiatives underway as a result of these brilliant influencers.

Expanding begins with the careful process of how you select people—not for tasks but for vision in their ability to contribute. It's your ability to give permission for people to fly, to ignite them to become interconnected and interdependent tribes motivated by a desire to see one another succeed, and for the company to succeed as a result. It's important for you to establish a system of accountability but not to do so in a silo. Remember that final metrics of client health, employee satisfaction, and ultimately company performance are inextricably interwoven. At the end of the day the growth of any organization is a people affair.

Checking the List

✓	Do you have a recruitment philosophy?
✓	Do you have an orientation process tied to your value system?
✓	What employee practices will you stop? Continue? Start?
✓	Do you conduct a staff survey?
✓	Do you link employee health measurements to your external performance?

CHAPTER 5

EVOLVING THE CLIENT MARRIAGE

HOW TO ADAPT TO EVER-CHANGING CUSTOMERS

"Without ownership you have nothing."

"You must be prepared to evolve your own self-belief."

Think back to when you began your entrepreneurial journey. Remember those early adopters, the folks who saw something special in you and had confidence in you? You know, the ones who were willing to throw their lot in with you, take a risk, and support your vision? You may still have them as clients. They were vital to your early business as they were the validators, those who helped you launch the rocket ship of your company and testified to the validity of what you were bringing to the world. These were the exemplars, and catalysts for others to follow, and the basis upon which the business was built. As I look back, I realize that our founding client was not a company, but people, individuals with two vitally important qualities: *ownership* and *competency*. These qualities were relevant when we started, and they continued to be critical as the company grew. As our company provided consulting in marketing communications—a true service business in an industry that has been going through significant disruption—both *ownership* and *competency* were critical to weathering stormy periods and to ensuring we never lost sight of what we were trying to accomplish. As you evolve, you will seek and attract an ever-increasing number of customers. It is my view that the qualities of *ownership* and *competency* should be the criteria for those you pursue as well as part of your quest in forging a productive relationship with others. More important is the role you play in ensuring your clients come to the table with both and, if they don't, knowing how to bring it out in them.

OWNERSHIP

Now, we were unique in the fact that we began with joint ownership as the foundation of our operating model. That is a commercial fact. When I refer to ownership, I am speaking of something deeper and more profound. It's emotional. It is an enlistment, a belief, a commitment to shared partnership. A great customer is one that feels a profound sense of pride and has stake in the joint undertaking. Ownership means customers do not see you as a purveyor, a supplier, or as merely being in a business transaction. Ownership is feeling they are on the same journey as you. They inherently believe in you, your business model, and the great things that can be achieved together. It is a relationship where your vision is shared, your value systems are in sync, and each believes that what you are setting out to accomplish is jointly held, doable, and desirable. Greatness comes from ownership.

A client without a sense of ownership sees you as a supplier. They have no vested interest in you or in what is being accomplished. It is a transaction. They pay you for some kind of output that is delivered, billed for, and that's that. Don't get me wrong—a lot of good work comes from these traditional relationships. But the likelihood of something great ever coming from a client/vendor relationship is significantly smaller, as there is no real emotional bond over shared ambitions.

COMPETENCY

The other element that makes for a complete, holistic, and highly effective client partner is competency. Of course, it's important that the client possess abilities in the practices relevant to the business—in our case, the elements of good quality marketing and advertising creation. But beyond this are bigger and broader skills of leadership, team-building, and advocacy. Creating a great idea is one thing, but bringing it to fruition is another. A client partner needs to possess a whole range of powerful business skills, many in the emotional intelligence arena, to create a following and bring your joint vision to reality. Ownership without competency will leave any organization short of what it seeks.

OUR FIRST OWNER

Our shared ownership business model was geared to drive a huge level of transformation on the client side and try to help them radically improve their marketing effectiveness and their efficiency. Kudos to everybody at JLR who had the guts and the will to build this or let us build it. The very first of our "ownership" clients was Adrian Hallmark. Adrian was (and is) a statesman. As the newly appointed Jaguar brand director, he met us for the first chemistry meeting and then subsequently for two setup meetings. From the beginning, Adrian was a big believer in the model. He felt this radical departure from the past would be a vital enabler to drive his success and the success of the Jaguar brand. He remembers: "The whole approach was about creating a backdrop to take Jaguar from a dusty, traditional, albeit respected, brand to five times the volume, and a new younger target audience in seven years without losing the loyalists. Our relevance to our existing agency or indeed any of the world-class groups was low. Maybe zero to five percent of their business. And while they talked about the value of Jaguar as a client, we had insufficient depth of thinking or talent on the brand. This is what drove us to set up a one-hundred-percent dedicated team, as an innovative joint venture, with world class talent—in keeping with the current zeitgeist of startup collaboration. But then it was very rare!"

He embraced it and he saw it—next to developing a future-focused product strategy—as a critical means. The new agency setup enabled him with a set of tools to drive change inside the worldwide organization in a way that allowed it to move fast to better results in a more efficient way. He set up all the right meetings, brought all the right people into a room at the time when the marketing department on the client side was small and still in its infancy. It was obvious that he had full ownership in our shared enterprise because it had huge meaning to him. It is no accident, as a consequence, that the landmark "Villains" campaign was developed during his time. He created the environment for it. Hiring Ian Armstrong as the Jaguar marketing communications director did a great deal for us. Ian, who had earned his stripes in the UK, let great work happen on the "Tango" and "Honda—The Power of Dreams" campaigns, with their respective agencies. Ian saw the "Villains" opportunity in a split-second. But, also, JLR the client team in the US under Andy Goss and our agency teams from the US and UK took that opportunity; the rest is history.

Adrian's ability to embrace a bold new initiative was born of ownership, but among his many competencies was the ability to pave the way and create the environment for success. We identified a number of elements that were really critical for success, and Adrian was critical in setting the stage. You may recall the reactions by some to the idea of "Villains" as the centerpiece of the brand campaign. Adrian never wavered. His steadfast belief in the concept against all doubts ensured it went from a vision to a reality. "I never felt like a client, but part of a quirky inner circle on a voyage, breaking many of the rules along the way. Ralf's team often said they were 'pirates' and after a time, I came to know exactly what they meant."

The next big disruption was the digital ecosystem, which we identified as a key priority. It was vital to make sure that the brand was able to compete in a marketplace that was driven by configurators and digital information. While at the beginning of the century car buyers visited five retailers on average before making a purchasing decision, that average had gone down to less than one and a half retailer visits, according to a study that Accenture published. The sea change was clear, and we could not lose a single moment.

"Well, let's go to work," he would say. Within eighteen months we delivered a new www.jaguar.com. Our internal name for it was JDX. (In the car industry everybody loves abbreviations—ours was short for Jaguar Digital Experience). This website created the basis for literally every effort we made, and became the pride of the agency and our client partners. In industry surveys such as Psyma's, it made it to the top three in all major markets, quite a way from where the previous system had been.

I still remember when the Jaguar folks came back from the presentation where the first Psyma results were presented. As this is an industry-syndicated study, all major brands were present at the workshop. Our colleagues from Jaguar were really proud, for all the right reasons. JDX ranked at the top of seventeen of the eighteen dimensions that were tested. One anecdote made it into the corridor conversations: The marketing director of one of the German premium competitors stood up during the meeting after fourteen dimensions were presented and said, "I just can't stand this. Everything you present, Jaguar is first." This major breakthrough allowed us to build a digital experience that was contemporary, that was relevant, and that made it a real advantage for the Jaguar brand in the marketplace.

Kudos go to a number of people, but one of our initial founders, a guy called Alastair Duncan, spearheaded that digital project together with Mo Sloane as the customer experience strategist. They made it work and got it off to a place where it became the number one website, and it wasn't just in the UK; it was doing very well in the majority of markets where it was tested, including on mobile devices.

Without question Adrian was a real advocate, a real ambassador, for us as a brand. He stood up at the Geneva Motor Show and presented the innovation that Spark44 was bringing to the table to automotive journalists during the press conference. He stayed with us as a brand director before he moved into another position at JLR in 2013.

DIFFERENT TIMES... DIFFERENT CLIENTS

The next big change came our way with the successor of Adrian's successor. The third CMO in only four years, Gerd Mäuser had been consulting with JLR when we started Spark44 in 2011. Since then, he had focused on a number of different things—like being the president of a Bundesliga football club. But when he returned to JLR as the chief marketing officer, he was a firm believer in the construct and understood the ability to drive efficiencies and drive governance through that model. He entered an owner. Little did we imagine what his competence would be and what impact it would have on us. Gerd is an organizational genius. He understands all of the moving parts, how to achieve operational excellence, how to structure processes, how to transport best practices and galvanize large global organizations around a common objective.

When we approached him with what we felt was the opportunity for JLR to consolidate all marketing communications (marcoms) globally with Spark44, he got it right away. One of his first decisions became this huge project of consolidation. His organization was surprised by the speed and rigor with which Gerd approached this gigantic activity. It goes without saying that when such a major undertaking gets kicked off, there are parts of the organization that have difficulty getting behind the idea. Gerd put all his weight behind the idea and got his marketing leadership around the world to accept it.

The internal code name was "Project River," and it was the most far-reaching decision in JLR's history in the marketing space. The sister brand to Jaguar at JLR, Land Rover, with over sixty agencies around the world, would be consolidated at Spark44.

When we were discussing the timeline, I remember JLR marketeers from all around the world were questioning the approach, but Gerd turned them down by saying, "These guys had done it on a smaller scale in four months for Jaguar—I have no doubts they will be able to make it happen in six months this time."

The transition of all advertising marketing services functions from all agencies across the world on the Land Rover brand started. We had to build all new offices, hire new people, transfer services, all seamlessly, without dropping the ball or missing a beat. One of our team said, "It's like redesigning a fighter jet while flying it." It happened: on July 1, 2015—only six months from first meeting to opening the offices and the full transition—my colleagues who were in charge welcomed their bigger teams or opened the doors in their newly built offices. And it has been delivering ever since.

It is fair to say that the transformation weighed heavily on infrastructure and on efficiencies. We all agreed that, over time, this had an impact on the creative side. We had not maintained the innovation that drove the "Villains" campaign for several reasons, and agreed unanimously that all of our energies had been diverted. The pendulum needed to swing back now that this herculean task had been completed. It took quite a while to put the energy back in the appropriate way and to help our client partner recognize that our single focus, as well as the reason for any amount of global infrastructure, is its ability to deliver brilliant creative work.

Not too long after this validation of the global/local, or *glocal* model (more on that soon), our office in Shanghai won a silver Effie for the relaunch of the Jaguar F-PACE crossover vehicle in China. This was a huge achievement because it was produced not by the usual suspects, London or New York, but from our newly created office in China. Coincidentally, one of the last pieces of work that Gerd signed off on was the Range Rover Dragon Challenge. This extraordinary torture test consisted of climbing 999 steps at a death-defying 45-degree angle. It began at the bottom of the Tianmen Mountain Road in the Hunan Province of China, which has an extraordinary stone stairway and ninety-nine dizzying turns.

The wonderful idea put us on the finalist list again for the US Effie, and we went on to capture the silver Effie. The groundbreaking piece of work, created by Chief Creative Officer Brian Fraser and the team, was a powerful demonstration that the Range Rover Sport was capable not only of navigating a serpentine road in the mountains of China faster than a Ferrari, but it was also the only vehicle so far—and probably ever—that climbed the 999 steps to the top of the Tianmen Mountain Road.

THE OWNERSHIP VACUUM

Now, it might seem that since the development of our company we have enjoyed an unbroken level of ownership from our clients. It must be said, however, that this has not always been the case. There have been individuals we have worked with, some with world-class talents, for whom ownership was not part of the mix. It is a remarkable, albeit painful, experience to see the negative effects they have on a global team of individuals. I have often asked myself the reasons for this, and I'm self-critical in trying to understand why I and my colleagues were unable to build a sense of ownership with some of these individuals from the beginning.

You could see the difference when you looked at the results both internally and externally. In the end, I determined the fault did not lie fully with us. Sometimes you have to fight uphill battles. If you are clear about the benefits you bring, make sure you hold the line.

But never forget the impact you have as an owner for your business. What would you be able to inspire with the same team, compared to a non-owner? Two completely different results.

The non-owners sew mistrust and an us-versus-them mentality, and leave demotivation in their wake. From my perspective it seems that there are a few reasons for this, not the least of which are fear, self-centeredness, and a lack of experience in matters of this scale.

The evidence is clear when you compare the groundbreaking results of the various owners I cited to many of the others who followed. What was common to these individuals was an abiding belief in the model, in the vision, in us as people, and in the value system that bound us not as client and agency but as one unified group of individuals in pursuit of an unprecedented objective. We began our journey with Adrian, who understood the vision and had an uncanny ability to bring people together around it. We had Gerd, whose marketing prowess was only exceeded by his extraordinary global organization design and talent management skills, about which textbooks could be written.

The lesson is profound and I think what we learned is to be prepared to listen. Somehow when you begin to achieve some level of success, the mistake many make is to think that as a result of that success you know better.

LESSONS FOR YOUR CLIENT RELATIONSHIPS

Think again. It is axiomatic that as you grow your company, you will grow with your clients, but also new customers will come to you. Some will come knocking on your door, and it's important to decide whether you wish to have them as clients or not. If you do, what steps will you take to build a sense of ownership, on one hand, and to allow these individuals to express their competency to the betterment and evolution of your company on the other? In summary, let these truths guide you:

1. *Ownership is everything.* No matter who comes into your world, they must be invested in you and what you seek. It's possible that they are not there from the very beginning, but you must work together to get to them to a good place. Without ownership you have nothing.

2. *You've got to listen.* You must be prepared to evolve your own self-belief and lose any xenophobia that stands in the way, to be open to listening and open to change as a new generation of clients comes to you.

3. *Seek new competencies.* Your evolution will call for different kinds of competencies. Be open to them, be receptive to them, and, perhaps more importantly, seek them. What worked for you yesterday is not going to work for you tomorrow.

4. *Cut your losses.* One of the qualities that I have observed as we have grown—and certainly in other organizations I have been a part of—is the tyranny that can occur from a client who lacks a sense of ownership. This is a true conundrum. On one hand, the customer might well control a significant amount of your revenue, and thereby your future. At the same time, a client who lacks ownership can be a corrosive force, demotivating to your people and ultimately a danger to the health and future of your company. Take a stand. Take steps to bring your client to a state of ownership. But be prepared to stand your ground, state your case, and, if need be, to stand in opposition to people whose lack of ownership may reduce the quality of your work. The future of your company is at stake.

Checking the List

✓	Is your entire leadership team really listening to your clients?
✓	Do you have a plan in place to extend the competencies of the firm?
✓	Have you found ways to ensure that your clients feel "ownership?"
✓	Are competency and ownership well balanced with your clients?
✓	How do you approach when either one is no longer balanced?

CHAPTER 6

TAKING ADVANTAGE OF A GOOD CRISIS

HOW A CRISIS BECOMES A MEANS TO PROPEL THE COMPANY TO THE NEXT STAGE

"You never let a serious crisis go to waste."

"What does not kill you makes you stronger."

There isn't a person in any organization of any kind that hasn't experienced some form of disappointment, setback, or crisis. I do not use these words interchangeably, because there is a difference between them, a continuum of sorts. Disappointments: well, we've all had those, sometimes daily or weekly, where circumstances just don't seem to go our way, only to be rectified by some positive occurrence that over time seems to even things out. The setback: well, that's a circumstance where our forward momentum is halted or stunted in some way, and, once again, after its resolution we carry on toward the destination we were headed for. A crisis: well, that's another thing altogether. The crisis is existential. The crisis is a circumstance in your journey that threatens the foundations of what you've built and believe me, you know it when you're there.

I've observed two forms of crisis in my career. There are those that you can see looming on the horizon, fundamental threats which many organizations see but do little about. Like the digital imaging transformation for Kodak or the mobile revolution for Nokia, these crises could be seen plainly and, if not for corporate inertia, averted. There are those crises, however, that are unforeseen. In many instances they are a perfect storm, the confluence of several events that conspire together, threatening your present and your future. I certainly hope that those of you reading this now never experience this, but likely, you will. The question before you: not only how to deal with the crisis itself, but, more importantly, how you can use it as a means to propel your company to the next stage.

It is a strange paradox that success for an entrepreneur and the achievement of many, if not all, of the initial goals of its founders and the establishment of a stable successful company can be the seeds of its destruction. One of the great mistakes that many businesspeople and entrepreneurs, in particular, make is believing that by achieving the creation and establishment of a successful business model, somehow their success will continue this way in perpetuity. The one thing you can count on is that the only constant is change. Context, business conditions, innovation, and external forces will all conspire to disrupt the order that you worked so hard to create.

A crisis is not a once-in-a-blue moon circumstance or a rogue activity that simply must be weathered. It is an inevitable circumstance born of a changing set of conditions. If this is true, then a primary role for any chief executive of any organization is *chief change agent*. I watched through the years how successful organizations calcified and hardened in their organizational structures, practices, and beliefs. The problem was, how could these organizations, enjoying current and near-term success, "blow themselves up" and change direction? It's exceedingly difficult to change an organization that is enjoying success versus one that is in decline. Successful organizations have significant internal resistance and stasis that make systemic change challenging. The crisis is catalytic. It provides a necessary wake-up call and a fundamental shift in circumstances that offers you an impetus, a motivation, a rallying point for your team, and an efficient opportunity to institute sweeping and profound changes in your company. It is best encapsulated in a comment by an American politician, Rahm Emanuel: "You never let a serious crisis go to waste. And what I mean by that is an opportunity to do things you think you could not do before."

THE PERFECT STORM

Seven years into the creation of Spark44 we were enjoying a good deal of success. In running any large multinational organization, disappointments and setbacks are ever-present. I would counsel my team that if everyday problems kill you, don't get into the kitchen. In an organization with nineteen offices and more than a thousand people, you can be sure that there's always something going wrong somewhere. Your role as CEO doesn't usually require you to get involved, because you chose a team that should be able to deal with the usual and customary setbacks. The question is, how do you figure out that there's a real crisis happening? It's sort of like a doctor in triage; you only find out when you listen, question, watch, read the signs, and understand them. Even if you think you've understood them, you find out later that you didn't really understand them while they were happening.

In September 2018, news was beginning to leak out that Jaguar Land Rover, our joint venture partner, would not meet their financial objectives. It seemed utterly unthinkable. The celebrated renaissance of Jaguar, the darling of luxury automotive, the perennial Land Rover with its highly successful following, was now faltering. The uncertainties caused by Brexit, the about-face in diesel vehicles dubbed Dieselgate, Chinese economic setbacks, all compounded by potential US auto tariff threats, conspired successfully. Jaguar and Land Rover sales in China took a serious hit, with no signs of abating. It became clear that it would have a major impact on their business and ours. Our joint venture partner had to turn over every stone to figure out how to improve their financial situation.

A TRANSFORMATIONAL CRISIS

I called for an extraordinary Finca Meeting the week before Christmas. We usually run these sessions as meetings among ourselves, where we discuss, agree, and take certain initiatives. This time, I didn't feel that was the right recipe for success. I thought we would need some more inspiration to deal with the challenge, because I thought not everybody yet understood how big the challenge was or how our partners were seeing it all.

I brought in two interesting people. First, Kieron Matthews from Flock Marketing Transformation Company, which is a company that consults with clients on how to improve their agency relationships. They had run the biggest and most successful agency pitches around the world, and I thought they could probably give us insight into how clients and agencies were structuring and what we could learn from that.

Kieron did an exercise with the whole team. First, he explained different structures, different approaches, different work methods, different setups. Then, we compared those to ours and tried to understand whether there was a total fit or where we could take elements of one or two or three of these setups and apply them. He got the entire team thinking about where we needed to take the company in order to drive our future forward. At the end of the session, he took me aside. What he shared with me made me enormously proud. "You know, your agency is very special. Agencies often think they are at the forefront of innovation. But interestingly, they often are very traditional. Our experience is in high demand with leading client organizations. But Spark44 is actually the first agency that has asked for our expertise—you are special and the way your team adapts to these different approaches is unique."

The second person we introduced was Neil Cassie from The Cassie Partnership. We brought him in because our communications director, Diane Scott, had worked with him in her previous role at Visa, where he had been tremendously helpful as Visa went through a significant restructuring and shift in focus. Both Diane and Ali

McManus, our global HR director, thought that we could use some help managing the behavioral side of what we were about to go through. Neil's session with the team focused on how people were feeling, communicating, and working together.

The sessions were held on day one in the afternoon, and on day two in the morning. Our group was split in two, and both became strong advocates for what they experienced and decided together. The Kieron Matthews group discussed and agreed on systemic organization changes. The Neil Cassie group centered on staffing issues, what kinds of people would be needed in the new order, a new communications structure to take people with us, and the need to say farewell to the people who could not stay with us any longer.

For me, it was a perfect result, because we achieved strong advocacy and buy-in for what we needed to do next. It allowed us to leave for Christmas with a clear mind and come back in the new year with a renewed focus on how to get it done. We didn't have much time because we knew that our client partners would announce their restructurings at a certain point in January, and we had to be in sync because of the joint venture structure. We had ten days to get our organizational structure moving forward, and I can say that without outside help we would never have been able to meet this challenge. The Lesson: Don't be afraid to enlist outside support. It's a sign of strength, not weakness.

A NEW PATH

A transformational crisis, if handled right, has the potential to be a significant step forward, even though there's pain that caused it. It means going beyond mere downsizing to a fundamental redesign that establishes an evolved entity that's fit for its purpose. The central premise of our restructure would revolve around shifting from a center-heavy model to a much more local-centric engagement, revolutionary in many ways for global brand management and advertising creation. It meant involving local offices in global matters, taking the lead on global initiatives. The center would be a leaner group, whose role would shift from concentration on all global advertising creation to becoming more one of guide, inspirer, and leader. The creation would be achieved by establishing local leads for each successive initiative. It became obvious that we had to make changes in the global leadership team as well as in local leadership. We would need people who could operate in a completely new way, and we felt that several people, while well-regarded and talented, did not possess the skillsets and experience necessary for the task ahead. This is an inevitable by-product of evolving. It is not a question of lack of talent; it is whether the skillset is ready for the new challenge. Some are; alas, others are not. Fortune had it that we had already changed the leaders in Shanghai and in Frankfurt with leaders who, on balance, would be ready for the task. Others would need to change.

We had two critical offices in which we had to make a change. One was our office in India. As India was also the home country of our joint venture partner's parent company, Tata, expectations ran high. Our initial new client relationships had started with Tata Global Beverages, and there were additional opportunities with the Tata Group coming up. We needed to be ready for these.

SAD GOODBYES

The US was the big question mark. We had run an East Coast–West Coast solution since our inception—spiritual homes of sorts, especially Los Angeles. It became abundantly clear that we had to consolidate both offices in New York. The bi-coastal office setup was less than desirable, not centered on the needs of the brand but on personnel issues, internal and legacy considerations, and emotions, which kept us from addressing what was to be a painful and messy restructure. The crisis forced us once and for all to break with the past and implement a solution with an efficient and effective organization design. We closed one of our founding offices in Los Angeles. Tony Hobley, our MD since 2015, had been through all the storms with me. I had to make one of the most difficult decisions: with all this change did we need a bigger change that would include the leadership team as well? The answer was yes. I had to say goodbye to a fine fellow, a colleague who had become a friend over the years. When he and I discussed the situation, Tony proved to be the gentleman I had always believed he was. His reaction was unbelievable when I shared my thinking. "Listen, Ralf, I get why you want to do this and I understand. Let me commit to support that change until the new leadership can start, because I believe in the spirit behind our agency." I was speechless, and my appreciation for the gentleman in Tony increased exponentially that day.

As your organization matures and weathers a crisis, it will call upon you to make tough choices. Emotions may at times get the better of you; however, the choices must be made, and for me, made with plenty of thought and compassion and as much support as possible for those who leave. I am pleased to report that, as of this writing, all have fared very well indeed.

TURNING TO THE MARKET

One of the downsides of an internal focus is the potential for taking your eyes off the marketplace. It was obvious that we had to get into a forward-thinking mode again, and not just be reactive. That's why it was so critical to me that all actions that were connected with that restructuring were to be finished and solved by March 31, or two months from it being made public, in order to refocus the company on where we needed to go. With service to Jaguar and Land Rover in place, I felt it was time, with the blessing and support of our joint venture partner, to pursue new clients to add to our portfolio. We developed what we call a "new balance" growth strategy to move 25 percent of our business over three years toward non-Jaguar Land Rover business. This news infused new energy and had the effect of giving our people an exciting new direction.

At the same time, we were busy working on Land Rover's most desired new vehicle launch, the new Defender. Both the work on that campaign and the new business initiative gave everybody a lot of hope, and the result was more than I could have hoped for. While we had a tough time in 2018, when we were already starting the collaboration with Master & Dynamic as well as Tata Global Beverages, we signed three pieces of new business in the first three months of the new fiscal year: Allianz Insurance, Tata Communications, and Harley-Davidson's international retail business.

All of those prestigious brands gave people a lot of hope and a lot of confidence that we were following the right strategy. By the end of May we had the opportunity to celebrate big in the US: the first Effie for the Land Rover brand in its entire history was ours. The marketing industry's highest honor for marketing excellence for the Dragon Challenge for Range Rover Sport—it was so important to us. We took the silver Effie home—in the automotive category no gold Effie was awarded, so this was the recognition for the most effective campaign in the automotive category in the US.

What we learned from this experience is that you can't plan for a crisis, but you can plan for what you do in response to it. Be clear about what you're going through; figure out where the North Star is for your people; make sure that you align your management toward that North Star and put people who are fit for the new purpose in charge; and bring as many people into the boat as you can.

WHAT ABOUT THE CAPTAIN?

I don't think the expression "the captain is the loneliest person on the ship" was ever clearer to me than in the dark days of the crisis. More than any other time in your leadership journey, eyes turn to you. There is so much expectation that you know exactly what's happening and why, that you have clarity on exactly what to do, while at the same time giving your people the sense that it will all come out well. I'm sure that many of you feel as I did, that you have none of the answers to these questions at the beginning and even at times during the resolving the crisis before you. I do believe that one province is indelibly yours: that you are a wellspring of confidence; also belief in your people and the communication that, though circumstances are difficult, it will all come out well, and the crisis will be successfully resolved. Your belief becomes their belief. It is a declaration of faith.

The answer to the question of how to deal with being the loneliest person on the ship was simple for me: You have to figure out how *not* to be the loneliest person on the ship. Crisis can be isolating, so I chose several ways to surround myself with people that were in the boat with me.

The first step is to figure out who are your best allies internally. I was lucky because I had Avanesh Sharma as our chief financial officer and Brian Fraser as our chief creative officer with me. Both were highly respected within the company, both were highly regarded by our client partners, and both were critical to making this mission work. I decided this "holy trinity," as some jokingly called it, would move through the crisis as one united leadership circle. It was great for me to have their invaluable insights but also to show there were no divisions among leadership.

I realized the way forward was not only to surround myself effectively, but also to formalize increased accountability among the management team. Rather than doing the normal summer Finca Meeting, which we always did in June or July, I called a special session and brought everybody together in Milan and shared everything, holding nothing back about the severity of our situation, our vision for the company, our business plan, and our strategy for the company. I made clear the hard road ahead and the difficult decisions that would need to be made. This time, however, I made it clear that I would not be solving these issues alone, but that the group assembled and everyone in the room would have new powers and new accountability. You could hear a pin drop in that room as I shared this new direction.

My rise to the CEO position at the company meant that the chief operating officer position I previously held was unoccupied. All assumed that a candidate would be secured. Avanesh, Brian, and I decided that the right move would be not to fill the position, but to divide the responsibilities of that position among the assembled leadership team, giving them both the authority and resources to implement what we needed to get done. The reaction was utterly galvanic. Not only was it clear that the strategy was right, but what I realized later was that the team internalized, through this move, the confidence that I had in them to implement our plan successfully.

DEFINING MOMENTS

I can say with confidence that there is no moment at any time of my career that was more defining for me personally or for the Spark44 organization than the crisis that we experienced together. What I can say is there is much that you can do to prepare for this eventuality. Take the time to have conversations with your immediate circle. Speak with them about the road ahead, game out what the potential storms might be, be transparent about the concerns you have about the future, and create the environment for them to share as well. Look at your organizational structure: Are you empowering your people enough? Are they fit and ready for the inevitable evolution of your firm? Above all, remember it is an act of faith—the faith that you have in yourself and, most importantly, in the people that you surround yourself with, those with whom you will weather the storm.

Checking the List

✓	Do you have a recent crisis you can reflect on?
✓	Do you have a plan for a crisis yet to come?
✓	Do you know who on your team will be involved?
✓	On reflection, what would you *not* do in your next crisis?
✓	Do you see a crisis or setback on the horizon? How are you planning for it?

CHAPTER 7

FOLLOW THE MONEY

BUILDING NEW KINDS OF CUSTOMER-FOCUSED INCENTIVES

"Alistair, you've been doing this for twenty-plus years, what do you think your role as CFO is?"

"I'm a liberating force for the company."

To begin this chapter on the financials is to look at this subject exactly the same way we looked at everything else when we set out on our journey . . . to reinvent the function. The above quote came from what an outsider might view as an unlikely source. Alistair Cook, a veteran financial executive and Scottish chartered accountant whom Alastair Duncan introduced to us five founding partners immediately after we got started, had "seen it all" during his many years at McCann and before that at Ammirati Puris Lintas and DMB&B. We were all in full agreement about making him our CFO and having him join us as one of the founding partners of Spark44. To work with this remarkable, self-effacing fellow was to bear witness to a combination of creativity and iron-willed discipline. When we planned the financial function, we started with a belief that it was not an administrative backwater, a complex and difficult-to-fathom control system, or a means to count the results of the company while the rest of us were busy doing cool entrepreneurial stuff. It's rocket fuel.

The role of finance is motivating the company, shaping its priorities and making sure that what is in the best interests of the company is supported. This may seem obvious, but remember, we were creating a company in contrast to a long-established industry with an operating model designed for agency profitability first and foremost. Clients were all too aware and resentful of this; transparency was the buzzword of the industry, and a number of independent in-depth reviews of the traditional agency and media buying model (including the K2 report eventually published somewhat later in 2016) were finally surfacing a number of previously fiercely protected and sensitive customs and practices and putting the facts on the table.

Among the key findings were a number of non-transparent business practices. Furthermore, the report revealed some undesirable systemic elements to some of the non-transparent behaviors. All of us had had our fair share of experiences with advertising holding company behemoths—namely IPG, Omnicom, Publicis, and WPP. Their model of managing a global business should not become ours; we wanted to do without finance being an overbearing, meddlesome, and altogether shortsighted entity which would have been entirely at odds with running a new creative business such as Spark44. For us, the whole financial team had to be critical enablers.

Steve's genius was to embark on the opportunity to build an agency for Jaguar and Land Rover, making the new entity not an exclusive Jaguar and Land Rover agency but a free-standing agency in its own right which would later on be able to attract other clients. A key decision was to set up the structure as a true joint venture holding company with 50-50 equity ownership with all the shared partnership benefits that would accrue. Client and agency relationships go through love and hate, through good and bad, through great times and tough times. Alistair's genius was to counter any transparency challenges with a clear open-book policy that gained us the early trust and confidence of the Jaguar Land Rover finance and procurement departments and their senior colleagues. Alistair was also a realist and a constant reminder to anyone in our offices around the world that when all the euphoria subsided, it would be important to have a serious and long-term buy-in from our client base. Being a Scotsman did help—such individuals being well-known for their financial acumen, for being polite and reserved but not afraid to be forthright and honest when necessary, and for their practical and down-to-earth approach to problems, both inside and outside their workplace.

Part of the winning formula was the full understanding of the transparency issues and the opportunities our business model created, which allowed us to turn them into an advantage. The presence of the Jaguar Land Rover CEO and other members of JLR's senior management on the joint venture board ensured that there was a regular conversation about the future of the company.

Under Alistair's stewardship and the involvement of our leadership team, we learned much. I can proudly say that our achievements in the financial arena were as much of a breakthrough as charging a Range Rover Sport up 999 steps. Okay, maybe not as sexy, but no less a vital part of the alchemy that made Spark44. So, for this chapter, I've built a checklist of my top ten financial tips and lessons as you navigate this next phase of your startup.

1. ESTABLISH UNASSAILABLE CREDIBILITY

If you want your finance team to be enablers and contributors, then they need a higher-order mission and purpose. Without this they become a department, with all that word implies. We had made the decision about the form of the company—a joint venture organization—but it begged the question, how do you build it and how does it function? In our case, because we had the rare opportunity to build the company simultaneously in four places at once, we were debating a lot with our joint venture partners about just how we should set it up.

We were building the company and growing at an astronomical rate, from eighty people in four offices on day one to two hundred fifty people in six offices in year three. And then nearly 700 people in twelve offices six months later. One could plainly see that the exponential consolidation of Land Rover's marketing agency structure would be a mammoth undertaking, from a procurement perspective.

The procurement folks at JLR would be tasked with vetting this global consolidation of some sixty agencies folded into one Spark44. This was all compounded by the expectation of additional efficiencies and cost savings as a by-product of the shared partners model. All in all, this was a procurement person's perfect storm.

It was clear to all of us that the transparent structure we had built would be the perfect starting point to manage this project. Alistair and his two key international reports at the time, Wilfried Huth (based in Frankfurt) and Hector Aguilar (based in Los Angeles), directed the team through all the various challenges of consolidating in more than twenty countries and setting up new offices in twelve—and, more importantly, ensured that their counterparts at JLR understood their shared fiduciary duties and responsibilities very quickly. All involved fused as one team, striving to make good on our shared-partners model outcome. When the process was finished, six months after it started, we took stock of what had been accomplished, and we had overachieved on every dimension.

The whole transition and setup of new offices had inevitably been a frenetic and stressful six months for all our staff (but particularly for our finance team) as not only had they been required to incorporate and set up new offices from scratch in some far-flung markets (Moscow, Johannesburg, Seoul, Tokyo, Mumbai, Singapore, and Dubai) but they had also been required to assimilate a significant number of new staff from the numerous incumbent WPP agencies who had been handling the Land Rover business in those markets historically. In these moments it is always good to know whom you can call to help you. My ex-boss Gunnar Wilmot connected me with Sorab Mistry, one of India's "Mad Men." He was happy to help and brought in a colleague by the name of Michael Courtenay; the two of them were our squad-team for the Middle and Far East. I also remembered a former colleague, Bernd Misske. Before he and I worked together in the early 2000s he was operating out of Brazil; he also enjoyed helping us set up our operation in Sao Paulo. Without going into too much detail, I will just say that these three gentlemen provided extensive and continuous contact with a number of local experts who helped us out on matters such as the acquisition of local marketing, media, and advertising licenses, the identification of and negotiation for appropriate real estate for these new offices, and, at the same time, helped us through the local minefields of HR and employment law—all of which took considerable time, which we did not have.

At the same time, we were necessarily involved with JLR senior management in some extremely tough fee negotiations, as the Land Rover account was a large amount of money by any measure and, as you would expect, the JLR procurement people were looking to achieve significant savings to justify this major transfer of responsibilities. Nevertheless, and after all was said and done, the JLR procurement people agreed that both joint venture parties had delivered an outstanding new structure at a competitive price and were pleased to declare with a high degree of confidence that "our job is done now" and that no further oversight from them would be required. The company decided to have their finance teams work directly with the agency instead of procurement to allow them to "fry bigger fish" in other areas outside our remit. Given the noise in the industry about transparency, this was a huge leap in terms of shared trust—something that even we had not dreamed would ever happen when we were starting out. This trust, beginning with Alistair's ability to establish and maintain a special relationship with the JLR finance people, has continued to this day.

2. DO THE RIGHT THING

One of the first and earliest tests of the value system of *be honest* was in the formation of the corporate entity itself. Since we were starting from scratch, we could pretty well design it in whatever way we wanted; our JV partner did not appear overly concerned with the proposed structure at that time. These days a global company can set itself up in a variety of ways—but for us it did not make any sense to base it anywhere else than in the UK. We weighed the financial savings against other factors such as the importance of close ties with the Jaguar Land Rover financial and marketing teams and a place at the top table with JLR senior management. We discussed all of this with our joint venture partner, and then took the decision to make the JV a limited holding company in the UK (which has since been shown to be an excellent decision given the continued low-tax environment for UK corporations), with all local agencies being incorporated as 100 percent subsidiaries of the parent, including those in historically difficult and protected markets such as China. This has ensured a closeness to both the brand and the senior JLR management team as well as a more symbiotic relationship with the Jaguar Land Rover financial people.

3. OPEN THE BOOKS

We consciously set up the company to be wholly transparent, but what did that really mean? Were we to share what we judged was shareable? Given the industry mistrust, and the JV partnership design, it meant total and complete openness. We wanted to make sure that everything we were dealing with was fully transparent and approved from day one and that the company as whole, as well as every individual office, would be audited on a regular basis. In addition, we asked to be part of Jaguar Land Rover's regular audit timetable, which, apart from ensuring complete openness, allowed for significant learning and improvements. Even if you think you've got it all figured out, there's always stuff that you don't know, or can learn from or use to your commercial advantage to save costs—for example, the sourcing or consolidation of certain services. Needless to say, we had a number of situations where the growth was so rapid that some things fell off the radar. The JLR audits, particularly in remote markets, flagged things we hadn't looked at closely, like IT security or ineffective procurement practices. They proved invaluable. Don't be afraid to have others look at your company. Think of audits not as a thing to ignore, avoid, or scrape through, but as a means to learn, grow, and advance.

4. DO MORE, REPORT LESS

One of the things that I was determined to change, which was the bane of my existence and of so many of us who had endured working for advertising holding companies, was the endless torrent of required reports. It seemed like people came out of the woodwork daily requesting the same information packaged in a different way, taking up 25 percent of my time at a minimum and sometimes for days on end. It used to amaze me to think, *what if this management and leadership time was devoted to the growth of the business and the health of the client?* This was in our minds when we looked at the financial reporting requirements for the Spark44 system.

The answer would be concentrated and disciplined planning and freedom for our managers. We worked assiduously with JLR to agree to a retained fee for a scope of work for a full fiscal year. We negotiated hard, but put it to bed, and then agreed not to touch it anymore unless material things changed upward or downward. This meant putting commercial administration high on the priority list for a certain period of time, and low on the priority list for the majority of the rest of the time, so that people could focus on the work. As a consequence, the office and account leads have never spent more than 5 to 10 percent of their time on financial administration. Compared to the sheer amount that many of us had spent with our previous agencies, it felt like heaven. Our people were free do what they loved and were great at, developing great work and communications programs on behalf of the Jaguar and Land Rover brands. The results speak volumes.

5. BUILD FOR SPEED

One of the things a financial organization becomes if it does not see itself as an enabler is a roadblock and a speed limiter for your company. When I think of the old finance setups I had worked with in my past, speed was the enemy of finance, or rather finance was rather the enemy of speed. We needed to be sure that the organizational design of the financial team was not one with layers of bureaucracy, with each layer slowing the process down. How did we do this? We kept it small. I will amend that... we kept it small and *bright*. We spent as much time and energy pursuing and attracting top talent for our finance team as we would for the top creative jobs. For us, they were equal in importance.

Initially, Alistair and I relied on the experience of two senior colleagues, Wilfried Huth, a BBDO-veteran who had run the finances of that group in Germany for decades and who joined us in the early days after his departure, and Hector Aguilar in the US, who had worked with Steve earlier. These two guys and Helen Coomber, who became our finance controller in the UK, were key individuals in establishing all the agency's new financial systems and managing the necessary local and consolidated spreadsheets which showed all actual and projected agency resources and fees, comparing these to their previous agency metrics over the entire six-month process of consolidation. This consolidated Fee and Resource spreadsheet became our bible. As you can imagine, there are lots of moving parts in a company where you have a number of separate and free-standing offices—which of course quickly mushroomed in size and complexity when we grew from four offices and eighty staff in 2011 to our current nineteen offices and head count of around a thousand staff. Yet we have always relied on this key spreadsheet. Needless to say, this had needed to be updated constantly as agency and client resources, global and local campaigns, and global and local fees were changed or amended at lightning speed; indeed, the most famous version of this document (Version 51, or "V51," of 2016) assumed legendary status within the finance community that year—albeit we all agreed we would try hard not to repeat the exercise in subsequent years. You need such geniuses when you want to succeed.

6. HIRE BUSINESSPEOPLE FIRST

Think carefully about the type of people who populate your financial team. See them as businesspeople first, and as accountants second. It is like asking a doctor not to look at the patient as a heart or spleen problem or complaint, but as a person with a first name. The perspective is wholly different—and *human*. A true finance player is also a businessperson who sees opportunity. They connect with customers. They weigh investment. They understand that money is a fuel and a tool to grow a business. They see all sides of the puzzle.

Steve, Alistair, and I always worked closely together. On one occasion, we had a conversation about succession and Alistair said, "Well, I know somebody who could probably help you moving forward when I'm no longer here, and that is Avanesh Sharma." Alistair advised me that Avanesh had one key capability or competency that he believed would help us significantly in the future growth of the agency—and that was his pure business acumen. When I first met Avanesh in a restaurant in Singapore back in 2015, my response to Alistair was, "You're right—he's amazing. Let's not wait, I think we should get him onboard and we'll just have to figure out what he's supposed to be doing in the near term. There's plenty to do around here."

At that time, we had just opened a number of new offices in new locations, and although I had a lot of confidence in the ability of the newly appointed MDs to be successful managers, there was still a question about the commercial acumen these people had. The majority of these new offices were based in the Asia Pacific region, covering pretty much all markets between Tokyo and Seoul in the east through Singapore, Mumbai, and on to Dubai in the west. Avanesh was based directly in the middle of the region in Singapore. Alistair and I decided it would be a good thing to keep him there. We knew that Alistair's retirement was a good three years away, so we decided to make Avanesh the regional CFO and the regional COO, and gave him one mission: to train our general managers and MDs in the region to be commercially savvy, which he did brilliantly. What this ensured was that when he moved into the position of global CFO, he had full business understanding and could have a point of view not only on individual offices, but also on team structures and everything else as well.

7. CONNECT FINANCE TO PEOPLE

Now imagine all the times in your career that you had someone who worked for you and you felt they deserved to be given a small token pay raise, say $200, only to have a finance person from some remote headquarters say, "No, we can't raise pay this quarter, or this fiscal year, any more—we need to save on costs." Worse, it was not unusual for this deserving person to then see the announcement of quarterly earnings, and healthy bonuses being paid out to the big cheeses. You knew instinctively that if you couldn't make that simple gesture, that highly valued person might well leave at the next opportunity. Our financial team's credo was simple—they saw themselves as investors in our people, and the primary ROI to be stewards of is ROP, that is, return on *people*.

As I was writing this, I had the pleasure of sending bonus letters for the previous financial year to every individual who is eligible. It always happens in summer at Spark44. Here's the email that Karen Hyman from Canada sent back. It said: "*Thank you very much, I am very grateful for your support and to work for such a progressive company. The changes you have made to management have already resulted in far better communication and open dialogue—most companies would continue the status quo, but Spark has made difficult and drastic decisions to ensure its future success. I know how fortunate I am to work for Spark44 and I will continue to work hard and be appreciative of our Bold, Brave, and Honest mantra.*"

What else can you wish for?

8. THINK LIKE AN INVESTOR

When I look back at all the painful moments of my previous experience and finance's role in it all, it certainly seems that one of these was when the organization was being squeezed at the end of the year; it was also when the earnings report was announced and all the bonuses were paid to people at the top of the company. Everybody would scratch their head, saying, "Well, wait a minute, what is wrong with this picture? They didn't even give me a Christmas turkey, let alone a bonus!"

When we started the company, Steve's initial logic was to make key employees shareholders of the company so they would benefit from whatever financial success the company had. The founding partners debated that approach and agreed that 5 percent of the entire staff should be granted options to become shareholders in Spark44. This became a big success. It did wonders for loyalty and dedication to the business. But you have to be prepared to make the tough choices; as soon as you launch such a program you need to ensure you have the criteria ready for who can benefit. Once a year we asked all our MDs and functional leads to identify individuals within their office or region whom they thought should be awarded share options. Selecting from those—because there were always more people on the list than the 5 percent approach could justify—has been an intensive task, but one that connects management with staff around the world in a very special view.

We as founding partners would always take the long view. None of us agreed to any salary other than what we had before the beginning, with the rest of the money channeled into our people. Our reward would come in time. Investing in our people would pay the ultimate dividend and, no matter what, it felt great because it was the right thing to do.

9. WALK THE WALK

When we first told JLR of our vision for "better, faster, cheaper," we knew we would have to make a personal commitment. We would not afford the usual executive privileges associated with the C-suite. You might think, here's an agency working for these two premium luxury brands, so they must live the life of Riley—well, well. Our focus was to manage cost very tightly—and travel was one key element in managing cost. So, for our first workshop with the folks at JLR, Steve made a very important decision: He booked all of us into the Best

Western Falstaff hotel in Leamington Spa. Without giving too many details away, I'll just say it was an experience that neither Steve, Alastair, Bruce, Werner, nor I will ever forget. Remarkable what £70 a night can buy you. It actually ensured that everybody understood the right principle in the very first place, that we would hold ourselves accountable just like everyone else. Believe me; they are all watching you, for better or for worse. By the way, the Best Western Falstaff hotel is actually quite lovely. Don't miss the breakfast.

Our financial people were mindful they had many mouths to feed. They had a duty of care to preserve our precious asset: our talent. There will always be things that will happen, and you might not have the income that you predicted. This means not only thinking conservatively in managing the money. It means planning for contingencies and demonstrating that when things go bad, the knee jerk isn't "head count." (Think of what a terrible, heartless phrase that is.) It really helps the spirit and the culture of the company if finance isn't the bad word in the company but is seen as a champion because of its behavior and effort on behalf of the team.

10. SHARE THE WEALTH

When we first set up the leadership of the company, they all got founding shares. At the same time, there were people who were there on day one that weren't part of the founding partners but who were quickly recognized by their peers as people who did an outstanding job. We all knew the company would be not be able to run that well if these people weren't around.

We agreed, as a principle, that 5 percent of the company's population should be shareholders to allow us to extend shares to those people deserving and essential to our success. Later, we established an Employee Benefit Trust as a marketplace for employees to trade their shares. We held the principle that we didn't want people who left the company to continue to be shareholders. We wanted the shareholders to be people who wanted to benefit while they were active in the company. When people with shares left the company, we required them to offer their shares for sale back to us, albeit at a very open, transparent and pre-agreed-on valuation formula based on the current and two previous years of consolidated agency earnings. Moving toward years six and seven, and with the company having more and more people, some said, "Well, I might need some of the money now because I want to buy a house or send my kid to college." We created a way for them to cash in their stock if they wanted to continue to live their lifestyles in the present. So, plan a way for your people to advance their lives while advancing their careers. It will pay you back in so many ways, and, I'll tell you, it was always a wonderful moment when those awards could be handed out.

The lessons are clear. Your finance organization is not a means for counting, punishing, or controlling. It is a propellant. This will always require a wholesale shift in how the function is defined, how it is staffed, and what it believes its role to be.

Checking the List

✓	Have you given the financial team a noble purpose?
✓	Have you staffed it with businesspeople?
✓	Have you created a culture of employee-centricity?
✓	Have you linked the financial practice to your customers' well-being?
✓	Have you made them investors rather than counters?

CHAPTER 8

MANAGING GLOBALLY

CREATING AN INTERDEPENDENT ORGANIZATION

"To do the best work of our lives."

"Actually, we got the world working together."

Crisscrossing the globe establishing an international presence for your growing company is probably one of the most exciting things you'll ever do. It certainly was for us. But one of the things that nagged me throughout the process was how we would go about establishing a far-flung empire and yet keep our soul. In going global, you'll face a vitally important dilemma: you will be adding new people as well as adding new cultures, all of which has the potential, in most instances unintended, to conspire to derail direction and alter your core reason for being and the cohesion that has marked your journey thus far.

There are several steps we took that showed us how to ensure that this would never be allowed to take place. In place of global chaos, a multinational community of highly diverse yet like-minded people made for an interdependent global operation. The previous chapter explored the importance of setting up a finance and reporting structure for our company; here we will speak about running the business on a global basis to ensure that everything you have set up is not only highly functional, but keeps the soul of your company flourishing.

EVOLVE

The initial premise, as we approached the management of our international network, was that things change, but we quickly realized that that was not the right premise. We often think of change as a point in time or a moment in time when something has to go from one place to another. The better word is *evolve,* because evolution is a constant organic process of *change in flow,* a never-ending process that is built into the fabric of the organization. It means ultimately that the international organization is accustomed to the process of constant improvement, of being self-critical within an infrastructure to manage that evolution. Evolution supports the entrepreneurial mindset in everyone. It means you will retain your entrepreneurial spirit, and not turn into a lumbering bureaucracy. Throughout the design of our global framework I thought of Darwin's sentiment, that the success of a species is not about being the strongest but being *most adaptable to change.*

As I look back, there were five key things that we did to build one of the most contemporary and successful international organizations in the marketing communications industry. While it all looks nice and orderly now, looking back, the process was organic, a bit crazy, chaotic at times, and, most importantly, always in motion. Evolution requires it. Here they are:

1. *Initiatives*
2. *Tools and practices*
3. *Product excellence*
4. *Collaboration*
5. *Backbone*

INITIATIVES

Despite the dramatic change that has characterized the business, economic, and societal environment of the twenty-first century, many organizations are still structured using postwar military industrial hierarchy. One only has to look to the classic organizational chart, and you'll see the silos by region and by specialization. While exceedingly efficient and orderly for the early twentieth century, this model is ill-equipped for today's environment that requires speed, nimbleness, efficiency, and maximum utilization of talent. Of course, the beginning point of organization design must contain some level of structure for specializations and regional coverage. What's required goes beyond the chart—to build a process and permission for groups of people to work horizontally across the organization such that people from different silos are in continual workflow. The answer was found in creating key global initiatives, but rather than have these led and executed at the center, we created work teams drawn from all over the organization globally.

Building global initiatives results in killing two birds with one stone. On one hand, you're setting out to solve a specific problem; on the other, you're creating a global community because you're structuring for people to work together across borders and across disciplines. In doing so you are achieving global consensus and workflow, giving practical meaning to the dual citizenship concept that we articulate in chapter 9. Your business type will inform the type of initiatives you create. Here are several we undertook:

Spark BnB

Great initiatives begin humbly, nearly always because inspired people just take their own actions. I do believe we created greater than average cultural permission for these to happen. Spark BnB, an exchange program giving our people license to work in our other offices for periods of time, began with two friends and colleagues. One was Gonzalo Ocio in Spain, who was running the Madrid office, and the other one was Leticia Thenard, who ran our Sao Paulo office. As it happened, there were a good deal of business reasons for commonality and lots of opportunity to do things together, so Gonzalo and Leticia developed a very good, informal working relationship. Leticia's husband is Spanish, so every now and then she had the opportunity to come to Madrid anyway, and she always leveraged that opportunity to see Gonzalo. They soon became fast friends. They realized that incredible productivity, creativity, and ideation came from their "temporary stays" and out of their Madrid encounters came an idea. As Gonzalo observed, "We thought, why are we just keeping this opportunity of doing things together to ourselves; why don't we open this up to all our staff?"

This inspired an initiative where Spark44 employees could work from another location for upward of two months, doing their own jobs but also immersing themselves in the local company. We published the opportunity on our intranet and the response was huge. People were excited at the prospect of spending two months in a different environment, working in a place where they probably had never been before, creating lasting bonds and powerful ideas with their colleagues. Employees would go from being someone in an email or on a video screen to being respected and cherished colleagues and, most of all, co-creators.

From the early fly-by visits of Leticia and Gonzalo emerged a program that already in the first two years has facilitated forty people spending time in other offices. Importantly, there was no bureaucratic process such as "This has to be signed off on by the CEO." People got their work done—period. It led to a different approach to working across borders, working across cultures, an informal way of leveraging work that was created in one place and is now being implemented in other places.

Word about this program and the creativity it engendered spread quickly. Three talented people who were running our southern hemisphere offices—Jasmin in Australia, Nicky in South Africa, and Leticia in Brazil—figured out that for whatever reason there were lots of opportunities to share their programs. I really think they just liked each other a good deal and there was a rock band chemistry. Jasmin would summarize it, "I just adore these two and they me. It was like one, plus one, plus one equaled a hundred!" You would probably think there are fundamental differences in the cultures, but in getting together they found common ground to make magic together.

Sparkapalooza

Our organization was focused on one client for most of its time. But the world around us was equally important, and we needed to find a way to ensure that inspiration from other areas was part of our culture. Too often, we spent endless hours working on client work, and as with any creative organization, you need to take a break to re-center on your creative purpose. So we globalized an initiative that Milind Raval started in Los Angeles in the early days of our existence. He called it Sparkapalooza, a name that people outside California did not get fully when they heard it for the first time. The name came from the concept of music festivals—where people can move from tent to tent, stage to stage, to experience what they want while still enjoying the cultural experience. So, combining Spark (from Spark44) and Palooza (from Lollapalooza), inspired the name. Ultimately, Sparkapalooza became part of the global Spark44 vernacular. What sounded like a party was actually a program of inspiration with internal speakers from around the world and guest speakers from relevant and interesting areas such as media, music, literature, arts, and academia, among others. I remember one of my visits to the LA office where Sparkapalooza was going on and during the entire week the office day got interrupted for keynotes, roundtables, and other forms of workshops. A great experience for all, including the party on one night of that week. You could call it training; I'd like to call it cultural glue with a meaning.

The idea quickly became known across the world. For smaller offices, we did share Sparkapaloozas, such as in Tokyo where the Korean and Japanese teams met for two days full of workshops and shared activities. Similarly, the Mumbai office and the Dubai office met in Dubai. Being true to our founding principles, we kept cost at a bare minimum; guest speakers did not ask for any fees but enjoyed the inspirational atmosphere within our offices.

Our London office, notoriously known for being a bit skeptical of cultural ideas, met the first Sparkapalooza with resistance. "We are too busy and don't have time—why are we doing this?" We created a curriculum where teams were randomly assigned, briefed on creating a campaign for a London-based nonprofit that helps disadvantaged women get on their feet. We had Tom Hooper and Mark Strong come in and give keynotes, and closed with our Christmas party. Several people came up and commented that this was the best week they'd had at Spark44, and it reminded them why they got into the business in the first place—creative collaboration.

The Accelerators

An accelerator program, as we defined it, was to create global initiatives around some sort of burning need or thing the company needed to innovate. It might be a new product or a process to cope with new realities. Whatever it was, the key was that the solution was devised by a virtual team drawn from multiple locations as one cohesive "horizontal" work group.

One accelerator program in particular was born out of the feeling that there were not enough digital product development initiatives in the system. We created that initiative to do two things. One, to solve a lapse we had digitally. Two, to bring people together behind a common goal and make that a global workforce imperative and work standard that could allow our global company to work in a more agile way. The team, drawn from seven offices, worked to fashion an appropriate global work tool. They agreed it would not be a patchwork of off-the-shelf platforms, but an entirely new creation, custom-fit for the kind of work we do and the manner in which we do it.

The effort was led by Ahmed Hasan, who connected with all the offices and brought in Tiffany Randall to coordinate things. His mission: to ensure that everybody was on the same level of understanding of potential opportunities and what the state of the art was, and then empowering teams to work on projects and initiatives to drive the quality of the digital work out there, which led to the number of awards that we won.

Our MD in Dubai at the time, Bernardo Jun, took this initiative to the next level. As a Korean born and raised in Spain, he became one of the globalist role models at Spark44. Starting in Spain, then moving to Singapore and later to Dubai, he knew that uniting the talent of the agency toward shared opportunities would trigger huge benefits. He took the accelerator to new heights. In 2018 he gathered ninety individuals (nearly 10 percent of our "population") for the initiative. He selected a number of coaches from various offices and together they created initiatives in what they called *tribes* that had the potential to blow our clients away with their creative plans in various areas of the business. The spirit behind all these ideas: "How can we bring additional value to our client partners?" As a founding partner eight years earlier, I took immense pride in seeing these teams working in various sprints to deliver cutting-edge work.

This one effort ignited similar efforts across offices. Whenever we had a situation that required a task force, or a spot team being set up, we used the infrastructure that the accelerator program had created, because people were just like, "Yeah, throw it at us; we'll come to you in a few days and bring you the solution."

TOOLS AND PRACTICES

The standards we set for ourselves required a constant focus on the quality of the work. Not only because we were stewards of two iconic British brands, but also as our ambition was to meet the high criteria that our peers would take for granted.

One of the most important objectives for our company, but perhaps one of our greatest dangers, was the quality of our work. The model we created was designed not only to create efficiencies and effectiveness but to provide the environment and cultural fuel to create industry-shattering marketing communications. A few years into the formation of our company, we experienced a lull in the breakthrough quality of our work following the now-famed "Villains" campaign. Examining potential causes, we realized that among them was a lack of common, inspired strategic practices. In my experience quality of work is a direct function of the quality of the strategic thinking; the right process has the capacity to inspire out-of-the-box thinking. The task: how we ensure that we use the same inspired strategic methodology in nineteen different places.

The Spark Plan

One of the other things we realized during this process was that we had one of the most talented collections of advertising strategic planners in the world. These highly experienced people, with great track records and drawn from the most admired companies in the world, had never had a platform to work together, or exchange ideas. Even more fundamentally, they didn't really know one another. We began the Spark Plan development initiative by bringing eight people from around our system to collaborate using all of their previous experiences to craft a blueprint that could drive, guide, and inspire our people to create breakthrough work. Once again, we asked Kevin Allen to moderate the team. The team decided to examine the strategic breakthroughs and methods that gave rise to two of the most iconic brand platforms of the last decade: MasterCard's "Priceless" campaign and Dove's "Real Beauty" advertising platform. Luckily, Kevin was directly involved in leading the "Priceless" campaign development and by serendipity was close friends with Daryl Fielding, who led the development of the Dove "Real Beauty" campaign. The methods that underpinned these strategic breakthroughs, combined with decades of experience across the assembled team, resulted in the Spark Plan, a three-part journey driven emotionally; there proved to be a global North Star for our work. It's no accident that we soon saw awards and recognition for our work. The "Dragon Challenge" work benefited from this strategic underpinning, as did all the work for the "70 Years of Land Rover" with the masterpiece "Land of Land Rovers" that *Adweek* in the US called "ad of the week," although it had not yet run in the US. And obviously the powerful work with Eva Green and a "real" Jaguar in the "A breed apart" campaign that was recognized as the only automotive campaign in the top ten in the UK by *Campaign* magazine.

PRODUCT EXCELLENCE

"You're only as good as your last piece of work." This creative industry adage presents an ongoing obligation to every agency manager: the next piece of work needs to be better. This really drives innovation and quality of product. From day one onward, our ambition has been to develop creative solutions that were the pride of the industry.

The Annual Yearbook

Once a year, we showcased our work in our Annual Yearbook, which we shared with all of our offices and client offices. Initially, the book was a record to show what our teams created across all offices. At one point, we took the decision to make it our "Best of" album. It did what it was supposed to do: create pride with everyone as clients saw the work they signed off as one of the best examples of work of the past year, and our teams wanted their work to be featured in the book.

When I wrote the foreword for the 2018 yearbook, I deliberately struck a balance between the creative achievement and our "backstage" success, like the seamless integration of both brand websites on one common platform allowing significant efficiencies and enabling improved technological solutions to ensure jaguar.com and landrover.com continued to be among the best-performing automotive websites. Everybody who has ever done something like this can imagine what it takes to deliver on time and under budget. I had to thank the people who made that possible in this semi-public format. While the yearbook took the form of a coffee-table book, we provided an online version to all our staff and all our clients to ensure everybody could celebrate the achievements.

The Awards

In the beginning, we consciously decided not to participate in the creative award show game as we felt it would take the focus away from our key reason for being: to provide faster, better and cheaper solutions for our client partners. The first exception happened when we decided to enter the "Good to Be Bad" Jaguar F-TYPE case into the North American Effies and later on the Global Effies, as discussed in chapter 2. That success created demand for more with our client partners.

On one of my visits to China, the new general manager said during our first meeting: "Let's create something spectacular and win an Effie in China, too." This "something spectacular" was the work for Jaguar F-PACE, which won the Shanghai office a silver Effie in China in 2017. Last but not least, the first Effie ever for Land Rover was through the "Dragon Challenge" in 2019, which the award jury summarized as "a courageous and breathtaking piece of work." Many more awards were to follow for this piece of work: 2x gold, 1x silver at British Arrows, a Big Award from *Campaign* magazine, a gold medal from the German Design Council, a gold medal from Creativepool, silver at the Brand Film Festival, and a "Best" at the International Motor Film Festival.

The Creative Challenge

Over my thirty years in the industry a lot of things have changed. One thing, though, has been constant: agency people are hardly ever satisfied with the client briefing. The reasons might be a topic for a psychologist; I chose to be more interested in getting rid of that excuse when it came to reviewing work.

The way we approached it was threefold: 1) we wrote the briefs by ourselves, 2) we received a committed budget for production from the central clients, and 3) we involved all teams worldwide. The result was magic. Usually, we generated four different briefs to ensure we got four to five offices working on each individual assignment. The office leader would present the work at our Finca Meeting, and a mixed jury of clients and agency leadership would decide what got produced. When we did it the first time, it exceeded everybody's expectation. The smaller offices from Africa, Asia, and Australia really used the opportunity to showcase their potential. One of the winners of the day was an idea from our London office for Range Rover Evoque: a social media film named *Speedbump*. A bigger-than-life speedbump was built in the center of London, eliciting amazing reactions from car drivers who could not pass over that speedbump given its sheer height. While everybody else got a bit desperate in figuring out how to continue their journey, a driver of an Evoque was way more relaxed. His Range Rover negotiated the speedbump with ease and continued on its way, leaving all people at that location speechless. By the end of 2019, this film had become Land Rover's most-watched film on YouTube ever, with more than 30 million views and counting.

COLLABORATION

Developing global initiatives brought with it a tremendous challenge. As visionary as our people were, they were accustomed to working in a certain way because the whole industry works differently with a focus on local or regional campaigns. The industry tended to develop ideas in silos, pitted against each other with somebody winning and somebody losing. Our concept was about pitching *together*. Strange as it may seem, collaboration has long been anathema to the industry. We needed to build collaboration, interdependence, and a culture of reciprocity.

Interdependence is where somebody starts the idea and the next one develops the idea and adds another element to it, and you add it all together. At the end of the day you never know who owns the idea in the first place because the team has shaped the idea because they were all working together to craft it. This is a principle that we have continued, because we felt the power of these work teams offered a springboard for ideas to be leveraged and taken to the next level. These early initiatives proved to be a creative exemplar not only for our company but also for the industry. This meant leaders showing the example of putting aside ego, not making themselves more important than the quality of the work. Everybody felt that the contribution they got from the other colleagues wasn't "somebody's taking the project away from me"; it was "together we're making it stronger."

That is what got us, at the end of the day, extraordinary work—and, happily, all of the Effie awards. Three for Jaguar, and one for Land Rover work in just eight years, which is incredible. None of the brands ever had Effies before. In the beginning everybody was joining with pretty much the same goal in mind: "Let's write history, let's put Jaguar back on the map." That objective had so much power that people knew that putting their ego up there wouldn't help, and they would be part of a team that was bigger than themselves.

BACKBONE

Managing globally requires a profound cultural shift. But there are some simple practical considerations as well. Chief among these is something that is not as sexy and inspired as some of the initiatives I've just discussed but is utterly vital for making the entire process happen: a common IT structure where everything talks to each other, and where you can just plug in, wherever you go. Many companies lament the fact that their global infrastructure is a patchwork. This simply can't be. All things must connect. All the simple things, like all offices having the same password for the Wi-Fi, so whenever you get somewhere, you are immediately able to work.

I think it's fair to say that sometimes people underestimate the importance of the backbone of an organization—the financial structure, the IT structure, and the project management structure. When we founded the company, Steve had one thing that he was very outspoken about: the IT structure. In his previous life he hated when he was traveling around the world and into offices and always had to carry lots of gear with him because his laptop used a different system than those in the offices he was visiting. He had to have all the cables and all the paraphernalia. He finally said, "We'll just do everything on Apple so wherever you go, you'll find somebody. . . . You can just plug in." You had the whole thing connected. It made life very, very easy from an IT perspective. Having a great

IT system allowed for the service space and the speed and everything for the valuable work we were moving across the globe.

We trained everybody to think and work in a new way. A simple but profound example was found in a simple phone call. One of our colleagues went overseas, and she came back with a thousand-euro phone bill for all the calls she had made. Embarrassed, she led the charge for global use of FaceTime for all mobile calls. The result: tens of thousands of dollars in savings, and a more emotionally connected team.

I still remember when one of our senior executives and I had our "six months review"; he was still overwhelmed with the fact that the use of technology at Spark44 was so much the norm, whereas in his previous life at a renowned London agency it was so much more the exception. That was 2015!

If you want to go global, you want to be able to see what everybody produces and what's happening everywhere. We developed SparkShare, the project management tool that every office and every project manager around the world uses. You can find every project; you can find every brief. The simple efficiency of knowing where everything is and knowing that it's always the latest version and you always find it there I think saved more than a million dollars in labor costs and ensured that there was an increased level of consistency.

	Checking the List
✓	What initiative have you started that will serve to unite your people?
✓	Do you have a collaborative culture currently?
✓	How would you ignite interdependence?
✓	Do you have shared working infrastructure that fosters collaboration?
✓	How do you foster teamwork?

CHAPTER 9

EXPANDING YOUR FOOTPRINT

ESTABLISHING NEW LOCATIONS, GOING GLOBAL, AND YET KEEPING YOUR SOUL

"Don't rest until you feel you got it right."

"It is much harder to do, and it does take longer, but when you look back you realize it did pay us dividends."

OLD AND NEW

I spent my early career in the advertising business at McCann Erickson, famed then and perhaps now for its longstanding reputation as a multinational powerhouse. Its origins can be traced to the growth after the war years of its relationship with Coca-Cola and the expansion of its agency network, following closely behind the establishment of Coca-Cola franchises in cities and countries around the world. This was a command-and-control, dots-on-a-map model in which decisions, direction, standards, and creation emanated from the center to the far-flung empire around the world. This was a distribution-based model consistent with a supply economy which was about ensuring the effective flow of products and services to a waiting customer. The role of the advertising agency offices was to take whatever ideas and material were developed from the center and to make necessary adjustments—what we used to call *adaptations*—to fit the local market. So, the famed Mean Joe Greene commercial that made Coke famous would find its way into local markets like India, only instead of a football player it would be adapted locally to feature a cricketer. The rules were clear and the penalties for transgressions severe. Offices had very little latitude to break from central direction. The role of a multinational account person was to ensure global cohesion and adherence to the central party line. Spark44 would be quite a departure from this well-worn and outdated international model.

We were a unique startup in that the intention of moving our small office footprint of four offices and eighty employees to be global was clear from the beginning. This meant, as with all aspects of our company, the spirit of boldness would inspire a wholly different view of how we would construct and administer our international network. Within year two of our existence, we began to plan and pursue the establishment of a multinational presence to serve the Jaguar business; this planning would be redoubled when the Land Rover account was awarded to us subsequent to the successes we enjoyed with Jaguar.

WHERE AND WHY

The decision as to where you should plant the flags of your international network is determined, in my view, entirely from following the business. I know of many organizations that established international offices before the business had started, with the idea that their business would expand from having established a base. This is a very expensive proposition and there is no certainty that the business will follow once you establish an office and infrastructure. The best way is to determine where your client or clients are headed and to establish a network of offices as a consequence of expanding your ability to serve them. This was the underpinning of how we built the Spark44 network of nineteen offices.

The founding partners of Spark44 were based in the UK, the US, and Germany. We were lucky that these coincided with vitally important markets for Jaguar. As such, it was logical that those three places would be the starting blocks of the company, but we also knew that we had to do something in China. It's one thing setting up a US domestic office or even an office in Western Europe, but China brings with it an entire array of interesting challenges, notably the need to work with partners. It can take up to two years to be granted a license to operate on your own. Working with a local partner is a means by which you can get up and running quickly. Needless to say, working with a third party like this brings a host of challenges, not the least of which is their track record and level of trustworthiness. We established a relationship with a partner in Shanghai and could service our client partners in China, too, from day one.

FINDING YOUR TEAM

Steve and I set out on our quest to build our Spark44 community, approaching it in our own special way. Steve went looking for or calling everybody that he had worked with previously to build a team that he thought he could rely on one hundred percent. I took a different approach, thinking I would do myself and the company a big favor by bringing in entirely new people with completely fresh perspectives, including those who were not born and raised in the classic advertising business. I did not embrace the idea of calling everyone that I've worked with in the past to see whether they would be up for this adventure. The marriage of these two approaches proved key to the innovative team we built.

While Steve was searching his connections for the Los Angeles office, I set about building the Frankfurt team by using various professional social media platforms to search for people who were qualified in terms of their marketing skills, language skills, and cultural and interpersonal abilities. You remember the story of the "mining marathon" from chapter 4.

Steve and I were looking for people who were able to express not just an interest but a passion for building something, and that became pretty visible very quickly in each interview because, at one point, there was a certain group of people that asked for a job description; we had done lots of things in our business plan, but we had never written a job description for anything. My response at the time was, "Well, we're building something from scratch and we're expecting a certain experience in certain professions, but we're actually inviting people to join us that feel that they would be able to write their own job description in the first three months." It was apparent that, for many, that freedom was too much freedom, so they said, "Well that's probably not for me." When I look back, it was surprising how many people required the certainty of a defined set of formalities being ready—offices, infrastructure and so on. We didn't have those, and we were proud of not having them; therefore, it was clear that these people would not be the right people for the endeavor that we were about to start.

BUILDING AN AGENCY IN CHINA

Starting a new ad agency in China is not possible if you have no track record or tax record for a minimum of three years somewhere else. In other words: if you are a startup from abroad, you better find a partner otherwise you cannot even start there. But that was only our "startup-interim" solution. For us, transparency was key in the setup of our joint venture. It was clear from the get-go that we would not be able to deliver the level of transparency that both we and our JV partner wanted through a partner agency. The endgame was clear from day one.

We needed our own license as a wholly foreign-owned company. There is a reason, though, that most companies open in China with a partner: getting a license is beyond difficult.

In the West you work within a clear set of rules. In China the set of rules exists, too, but they only *look* straightforward. Once you are familiar with them you learn that every city district has its own special rules and laws. And you don't get your license without an office. We had to find an office in an area that would even allow us to apply for a license, promised success, and would welcome us. You can imagine us Europeans and Americans thinking this would be a never-ending story. But help was around the corner, even in the Far East. We found a small business consultancy that helped us work through the regulations and all the local offices involved. Obviously, navigating the timelines, papers, and costs was critical, too. But, above everything else, we needed patience: what we were told one day wasn't accurate the next day. Barbara Hans, who joined us early on to run the account in our partner agency, was on her way to becoming the managing director of a wholly owned subsidiary: Spark44 Shanghai.

Once you believe you have it all sorted, wait for what is around the corner.

Finally, the big day was here. All of "our" employees—as they were employed by our partner agency—were excited to sign their new contracts, the first Spark44 contracts. We had flown in our HR director from the UK to support. She and Barbara had discussed every person's remuneration. But she had not operated in this country before. So, what needed to happen happened. It was the usual local practice at the time to have an employment contract that showed all numbers in net as the company was looking after your taxes and social insurance. Barbara had told her and asked that she add taxes and other deductions, since we intended to apply the global contract version, which showed gross figures instead of net. Our HR director at the time had worked out the contracts overnight, headed back to Pudong Airport, and was on her way back to the UK with the last flight.

When Barbara read the contracts one by one to check all Chinese names and any personal details, she was shocked when she realized the numbers reflected the gross, rather than the net. The net numbers contract was such a foreign concept to her that she had not trusted Barbara's advice. All twenty contracts were wrong. Alistair, our CFO, every now and then surprised us by sending us emails in the middle of the night. This time it was a blessing. That night he could not sleep and picked up Barbara's call for help very, very early in the UK. He promised to get the contracts back to Barbara within hours. And he did. Barbara was able to hand out the right contracts to everyone at lunchtime. Happy faces all around—and only a few of us knew what had happened that night.

ACQUIRING DOWN UNDER

In 2014 we had the opportunity to extend our services beyond Jaguar, to Land Rover. It propelled our need to expand our footprint, including a strong presence in Australia. At first glance, the opportunity seemed easy because Australia was supported by a local agency that had been servicing Land Rover for over twenty years. Michael Winkler, the local JLR managing director at the time, approached me after a visit where I took him through the thinking behind Spark44: "Ralf, I have a crazy idea, are you up for it?" Of course, I was—so Michael put me in touch with a gentleman by the name of David Morris, a renowned creative director in Sydney who had built an agency beginning in 1997. He was ready to retire and said there would be an opportunity for us to acquire his agency.

Acquisition is a sound way of building a company. A good acquisition provides you an instant footprint and infrastructure with an ability to hit the ground running, with the bonus of potentially achieving profitability and performance from the very beginning. Acquisition, however, can be fraught with challenges, not the least of which is making the right cultural choice. Inevitably, cultural compatibility is the most important determinant of whether the acquisition will work over time. From my perspective as we were building a new model, I determined that it was against our best interests to bring an entirely separate corporate culture and operating system to our model, so set out to build our network organically. We didn't want simply to make an outright purchase in Australia, but to be more selective about what we would build and who would be part of it. It's much harder to do and it does take longer, but as I look back it certainly did pay us dividends.

I remember my first visit to Sydney, before I met David. We had a great Australian guy, Daniel Bevins, who joined our Frankfurt-based account team after his stint in Paris. When I told him that I was planning to go to Sydney, he told me "You have to meet my dad." His father, John Bevins, had been inducted into the Australian AdNews Hall of Fame in 2011. When he and I met for breakfast at the Shangri-La we had a real good time. He told me about this guy David Morris whom he felt I should meet—"He is a real pro!"—as he was running this independent Land Rover agency at the time. There was no time to meet him at that visit, but little did I know that David and I were going to meet within the next year, and more than once.

David and I met several times and I determined almost immediately that David shared our cultural sensibilities and that some kind of partnership would make sense, but it would not take the form of an outright acquisition. "John was right," was going through my head. We would establish a managing director, and hire select people from his firm that were consistent with our values and needs, along with others from the marketplace. As part of the deal with David we would construct an appropriate and well-deserved exit package for him.

Five finalist candidates for the managing director position were identified, and I flew to Sydney and interviewed them all. On the evening of the last interviews, David and I had dinner; we looked at each other, and I said, "Well, they're great, but they're not it." He said, "I know, I saw it in your face during all the interviews, and I realized perhaps the reason for the lack of fit was I was looking for my successor, but you were actually looking for somebody who carries the Spark44 flame into Australia, and these might be two separate things." I suggested we hire a headhunter and give him our *be bold, be brave, be honest* brief, and launch our search from there. I will always remember David's statesmanlike approach, but, most importantly, I'll recall his recognition that I was looking for a candidate more in line with our values than with his sentiment for his former agency.

After I made another long trip to Sydney two or three weeks later, we met another four candidates and again we had dinner in the same place. David looked at me at that dinner and said, "So, you're looking different today than you looked three weeks ago." I said, "Yes, because interview number two"—a woman named Jasmin Bedir—"was by far the winning candidate, and I hope you think so, too." David agreed that it had to be my decision, not his. "This is your future, Ralf, not mine. If you think she's right, go for it. She's German/Australian, a good combination, and you are wearing the same brand of watch, a good omen!" He also saw that this woman's boundless energy and can-do attitude would be a perfect fit. It was . . . and still is.

IT'S A PERCENTAGE GAME

You may well be setting up your international network with as rapid a pace as we were, adding new offices every few months. As careful and as disciplined and as true to your values as you make the search process, the law of averages will apply and not all of them will work out. The key is to take your time in getting who you think the right person is and to act fast if you discover they are not the right fit. Don't agonize or second-guess yourself; it's all part of the process. The key is, don't delay the decision. It will cost you if you do.

As we were building our network, I was relying on one individual who was recommended to me by our then client. I vetted him and concluded he would be helpful in assisting with setting up the offices and identifying the leadership. He knew the industry in the country and appeared to have all the right connections. All of this happened while we opened twelve new offices around the world. Oddly enough, the one that took us the longest to open up was right in my own European backyard, in Italy. The guy I was recommended soon turned out to be very old school; the office leader he recommended was a total miss. This became obvious after six weeks. This was a bad decision. You might think that I would wait a bit longer to see if it turned around, rather than face what might be an embarrassing mistake, but I didn't. Listen to your gut. If it doesn't feel right, do something about it. No matter how many times it takes, don't rest until you feel you got it right. When I sat down with the Italian client, Marco Santucci, at the time, he fully understood. We were good to move on with our new MD, Antonio Anfossi. The right decision from day one.

REPLACING CULTURE

Everyone you bring to the international table will have two important cultural biases, the corporate culture that they came from and the cultural filter of their nationality. The task for you is to bring about a cultural glue that transcends these differences and holds the group together. People joined us for the opportunity to rewrite history for one of the most iconic brands in the automotive industry with Jaguar, in an agency structure that had never been done before. We were able to excite people when we were talking about what to expect, a twenty-first-century company that would avoid all the traps and all the misfortunes that we had experienced in our previous lives in the big holding companies, the biggest one being a single P&L across the world. My discovery, though, was profound: I learned that people come to you for the ambition, but they stay for the culture.

I'll be the first to admit that in the frenzy of the multi-office development we didn't think of values so much; we felt that would come later, but it became obvious in a few short months that that thinking was shortsighted. We were all connected by the design elements of the new structure such as shared space, one P&L, no silos—an innovative company avoiding the mistakes that we had all experienced—but that wasn't enough. I realized the glue that holds a company together internationally is not process but values, and we moved very quickly to create a bonded community around our values of *be bold, be brave,* and *be honest.* We drove the assimilation of these beliefs and accompanying practices, office by office, and, in doing so, we turned a far-flung group of isolated markets into a cohesive Spark44 citizenship. It became clear that my number one job was deep quality time in each office, not necessarily from a COO-running-the-business perspective but as chief belief officer.

WHERE ARE YOUR HEADQUARTERS?

The most common question people will ask the head of a multinational enterprise is, "So where are your headquarters?" I always relish the looks on their faces when I say, "We don't have one." Building a twenty-first-century company meant parting with terminology and structures of the command-and-control international network days. We decided early that leaving behind the idea that every company needs a headquarters would drive an alternative culture based on being a community of generosity of spirit in values and interdependence in skillset. We invested heavily in digital work platforms, conference tools, and day-to-day individual communications with FaceTime, for example, replacing the common phone call. We built a nervous system connecting all of our infrastructure intuitively. Using technology for running the business and bringing people together was an extremely important part of our setup, because you can't replace human interaction with phone calls; you can't build trust on an email.

THE SPECIALIST MODEL

Among the many things we were keen to avoid was the dots-on-a-map model, each office a carbon copy of the others. We had neither the need nor the appetite to establish a full range of capabilities in each of our operating offices. Instead, we opted to analyze the unique capabilities available in these markets and establish a series of specialist capabilities in each of our office areas, identifying four offices—US, UK, China, and Germany—where the large-scale strategic program planning would take place. The balance of our offices would serve local needs, but would also house a particular specialty as well as a creative team that would support global programs as well as local activities. The result was extraordinary, allowing us to build a capability like we did in Birmingham, specialists who were capable of producing the highest quality websites, brochure collateral, and other sales support competencies in one efficient location. While these folks were doing their marvelous thing, another office, like Spain, specialized in contemporary social media marketing and another office led us globally in search engine optimization. This allowed us to have concentrated best-of-show communications capabilities without duplicating these efforts and markets throughout the world. At the same time, the local offices were participating on a global level while wearing their traditional hats, identifying and tailoring global communications for local nuances and marketplace needs.

We created forums for these functional groups and by doing so got the whole organization talking to one another, so the functional lead for retail marketing was talking to the key people who were focused on retail work, as an example, whether it was in China or the US. Very quickly people learned how the different car markets worked around the world. The offices were like planets in a solar system, each robust in its own way, revolving around a bright center. The global team management provided direction, evangelized corporate values, and assimilated these myriad specializations into a greater collaborative whole. Results for the client: complete seamless integration.

TECH BONES

A strange accepted wisdom in my previous experience was to build an organization and then attempt to "wire in the technology" after the fact. It seemed to me very much like designing and building a house and only figuring out how to run the wiring and plumbing after the structure has been built. For us the use of advanced operating technology at the company was a key element from the outset. Many newcomers had to unlearn previous behavior, for instance no longer using a cell phone to make "traditional" phone calls but using FaceTime instead. While many came from sophisticated places, I think it's fair to say everybody was surprised about how relatively old-fashioned work practices were at the places they came from. We were determined to establish an entirely different working system from the beginning.

There were some practical considerations that offered a bit of serendipity in driving the new methods of communicating and operating, namely, our three operating partners were in four locales: Los Angeles, London, Shanghai, and Frankfurt. So, if you have a chief exec that lives in LA, that makes life a bit difficult for anybody not living in California to connect. You're always nine hours away from everything, which puts you into either very early hours or very late hours, and that makes it tricky. At the same time, because the founders had to set up the hub offices and run them, it was just not possible to have all of us at the same place at the same time, except for certain meetings. We also had to deal with a client situation, with our Jaguar Land Rover partner based in the UK. We felt that in order to support the ambitions of our partner—the transformation that they had to go through moving from a UK wholesale company to becoming a global premium brand—it was vital not to structure the company with the UK as the center of the universe creating a "UK and the rest of the world" mentality. Robust connectivity via digital communications technology put the key geographies on equal footing and allowed for the seamless flow of global solutions rather than UK solutions for the world.

But operating globally also has some very down-to-earth facets. When it comes to implementation and execution, be prepared for some surprises along the way. Barbara Hans reminded me of one of the instances where she nearly lost her cool in Shanghai. Imagine helping your client with launching a new sports car in a non-sports-car market for a brand without heritage at all—Jaguar in China. So, you are trying to add the heritage that all Brits would associate with Jaguar by leveraging their historic products from the '50s or '60s. You bring in a famous photographer from the US who is capable of marrying heritage with the present. The Chinese client assigned an adequate budget, so off we went. Flights were booked; the whole machinery was put into action. But then the unexpected happened—the photographer had overlooked that for him to get paid he needed to have a bank account in China, which he did not. The implication: If you are transferring funds to countries outside of China, you pay a hefty tax of 17 percent. So Barbara and her team went into significant renegotiations to ensure the shoot was on quality and on budget. This shows that you need to be aware of every detail and have your eyes everywhere to ensure your operation runs smoothly and your teams are not distracted by things that are happening along the sidelines.

Managing the global enterprise through the use of modern communications technology replaced a lot of the old methods like boarding airplanes, but from my perspective was never a complete replacement for a regular flow of "human capital" between offices. At the end of the day there is nothing that replaces human connection between people who build relationships of trust and interdependency that can only come through close-up human interaction. Creating sensitivity and a balance of the requirements of the global organization and its marketing communication solutions meant taking advantage of the different nuances and opportunities afforded by integrating a local narrative in order to accomplish market success. It was vitally important on a practical level for the team to develop a hands-on working knowledge of differing local cultures. The American team had to learn about European cultures, Chinese cultures, the Chinese team. We were eager to understand how premium brands from Europe or the US were managed. For the UK team it was critical to understand the market behaviors outside the home market. In these early years the knowledge transfer of understanding international cultures as well as the behavior of luxury automobile buyers in our various marketplaces was critical. It's fair to say that we spent a disproportionate amount of time in international travel in that first year, with Steve spending a good deal of his time in China and me taking care of practically everywhere else. The implications for any entrepreneur building an international network are these:

1. Build a contemporary information technology-based communications and knowledge transfer infrastructure in parallel with the establishment of your network . . . not after.
2. Apply old-fashioned "shoe leather" to be present in all of your key markets for as long as it takes to get them established correctly and connected to the remainder of the network fluidly.

DUAL CITIZENSHIP

One of the undesirable characteristics of a command-and-control international network is the residual attitude between those at the center and those in the local markets. In this setup, it becomes clear relatively quickly that the only thing that matters is what happens at the center. For us who had lived these experiences, it was vitally important to build a network of egalitarian units, each of which possessed what we called "dual citizenship." First, each individual in each office had a role to play as an advocate for the global initiative that we all had a fiduciary duty to support on behalf of our client. Second, they would also be a "citizen" of the local market with an additional fiduciary duty to represent the unique marketplace nuances and important differences that had to be fed back to center to allow local communications. This dual responsibility would have the result of ensuring that valid local considerations would be aired, especially for markets that might not have a loud enough voice to state their case.

When you're establishing a global premium brand or revitalizing a global premium brand, global consistency is key. However, you've got to make sure it works with all the nuances in different cultures. We had to adapt our message to the Middle East, Asia, Russia, Latin America, the US, the UK, or Europe. Dual citizenship would ensure that these nuances were understood and considered before the solution was shared.

In growing up at McCann I remember a phrase, in McCann's well-recognized earthy manner: "Lead, follow, or get the hell out of the way!" If you want to run a global brand, you still have the "lead" and the "follow" pieces, but the key element of what we call the dual citizenship approach was to make sure that everybody felt a responsibility to state his or her case when it really mattered and made sure the leadership of the company "got the hell out of the way" for the benefit of the local market and the success of Jaguar and Land Rover in each market they competed in.

LEADING FROM AFAR

The final piece is when an entrepreneur who may have been running an organization of fifty people that they could see day-to-day, now has three, four, five, six, ten offices. How do you get comfortable letting go? When do you stick your nose in and micromanage? When do you stay out? Maybe, for someone like yourself, it's second nature, but how does an entrepreneur get comfortable with that? Are there any tips for doing so?

Obviously, I think you can only get comfortable with it when you have a trustworthy relationship with individuals in the other part of the world. The real question is, how do you get to a trustworthy relationship? As everybody knows, you can only earn the trust, and that works both ways. Everybody needs to invest a lot of time and a lot of energy and needs to be conscious that this is what needs to happen.

In the early years, we had ten or twelve people sitting in South Korea, Japan, Australia, Latin America, Brazil, and, even with the best will in the world, I wasn't able to give them more than two visits a year for one or two days. For many of them, it was one visit a year for, probably, two days per visit. So, there wasn't much time, you needed to really spend the time with the individuals and make sure they had a connection into the organization beyond you. Put yourself in the shoes of those people. They're a twelve-hour flight away, with local demands that they have to deal with, with remote support, and still, they had to make it work. That's a tough job. That's probably an even tougher job than for the one who's directing it. That's the way I've always looked at it.

All those people have my full admiration for what they did for us in those early years, and what they've been continuing to do in the later years.

If you've built the trust, and you've picked the right people, and people are honest about what's going on and share with you what matters, you've got a fair chance that this could work. But obviously, not everybody's like that, and sometimes you fail yourself, and situations arise where it becomes obvious that it doesn't work. Then you have to figure out what the cause is. Again, it's about trust. So, who are the people you can trust? You've got the client organization, who've got their own agenda, but still, even at that level, you've got to build relationships of trust in which people can have an honest conversation with you, and you can have an honest conversation with them.

That obviously works well with some, all right with some others, and not well with others. But if you don't find a way to communicate effectively with all of them you will not succeed. During one of my visits to Australia, my colleague Jasmin took me aside. She said, "While you are here, I would like you to join a GoToMeeting with Nicky from Johannesburg, Gonzalo from Madrid, and Bernardo from Dubai." They had some profound concerns about the way our team at the center was running their projects—and also about the fact that there was so much going on that they weren't aware of. Long story short—when I got home, I discussed the issue with our leadership and got back to those four with a solution that has become real ever since that Wednesday evening in 2016. It's called "Let's Talk" and is a monthly web-meeting with the executive team and all office heads worldwide where all current topics from a central and local perspective are on the table. Face-to-face (at least via the webcam). It helps a lot when you can see the facial reaction of your team—and they can see yours—when critical topics are being discussed.

Checking the List

- ✓ What is the true reason for expanding your footprint?
- ✓ How do you plan to promulgate your culture in new locations?
- ✓ How does expansion affect your day-to-day role?
- ✓ How often and in what capacity should you visit locations?
- ✓ How much freedom of action should they have?

CHAPTER 10

CREATING YOUR LEGACY

UNDERSTANDING WHAT YOU'RE BUILDING, WHAT YOU'RE LEAVING, AND YOUR EXIT STRATEGY BY REFLECTING ON THE FOUR TYPOLOGIES OF "LEAVERS"

"It's been the best job of my life."

"I am sure the future will be bright for all of you."

Looking back, if I had to summarize, there are two or three things that really stick out in my mind that would be the best advice I could give to you, the entrepreneur, as you set out to scale your business.

In every business, there are hard facts and there are soft facts, and, make no mistake, the soft facts are equal to and, at times, far more important than the hard ones. At the end of the day, it's all about the people. It's about them and the culture that you build, and your responsibility in protecting it. Protecting the culture, I think, is critical—but before you can protect it, you need to define it. I think the biggest thing you can learn is to build a foundation on the basis of clear values and establish a few things that people recognize as cornerstones of that culture. For us it was, to be sure, the starting point and reference for everything.

First, focus on your customers, because without customers there is no business. I know that sounds obvious, but the many distractions of building a company and the internal stuff that is involved can take your eye completely off the ball. In our special case, we had to deal with a number of key customers changing quite a few times. You always need to find a way to continuously build relationships with those customers, and, like Darwin said, success goes to those most adaptable to change.

You have to make sure that your team is fit for that audience, that they understand what the big picture is and what their role is at any given moment. This is especially true when times get tough—and, inevitably, they will. You need to be the one that helps your team with direction and with focus, but also with reassurance. Although nobody will ever ask you to "protect" them, what they ask for is shelter in the storm and that's what you need to give them.

Culture, the *relationship*, the *protection*, and the *direction* are the four key components, and as I have set out to show over the previous chapters, you need to institutionalize these components, so that as the company grows, they'll be qualities people can refer to (like the Larrys). The more things that are common and the more things that are identifiable as cultural markers, the easier it is for your people to get their act, their heads, and their actions together—cohesively. Something else to add to that list is, just remember that a setback isn't a disaster. It's a tremendous opportunity for you, provided you stay above it and treat it as such. Remember to understand what your center is, what you're great at, and remember that the only way you get things done is by understanding your strengths and your shortcomings, and ensuring you're building an effective, interdependent team.

There's a wonderful quote from Steve Jobs in his 2005 commencement speech at Stanford University. He said, "You can't connect the dots looking forward; you can only connect them looking backward." But as you're moving forward, you have to make decisions. As your company is growing and as your company is developing, there is no such thing as a steady northward curve. There are always ups and downs, and those downs are hard to deal with, because they always bring you to a place where you have to make tough choices. Very often, they affect the people you are close with.

Your function as chief executive is to put the well-being of the enterprise above everything else. Sometimes it's tough, and sometimes people look at you and think, how could he ever do this? You'll need to find a way to make people understand why you did things. It's often difficult to find the appropriate narrative, because you will very often feel that there are certain things you can't actually tell people. You have to find a way to share as much as you can, to allow people to understand what's coming and what's to be expected. When in doubt, communicate.

Find a good way to support and challenge at the same time. You'll be surprised how much you can challenge, because a lot of people actually love it, as long as they feel trust is there and support is there and the challenge is somewhat achievable. It might be a stretch, but believe me, they can do it, and feel amazing when they've done so. By the way, that applies to you, too. Understand what your strengths are, what your weaknesses are, what you're good at, and what somebody else is good at. Make sure that you are ahead of the game and understand how all the pieces fit together. It doesn't mean that you need to put together every piece by yourself.

Every entrepreneur experiences the early phase where you know everybody, you know everything, and you're part of nearly every conversation. Then, in a blink of an eye, you're big. Conventional wisdom is that when a company grows beyond a hundred and twenty people, you stop knowing everybody by name, and that's when everything changes. In this stage, you need to figure out how you can connect with your people, and a regular emailing program, video blog, or newsletter can work wonders. Make sure you have a platform to chat with your people, reinforcing what you believe and where your organization is heading. Try a coordinated event. We ran what we called Sparkapalooza, where all around the word, we would celebrate our successes and plan for the future. Each office would hold a multi-day program of activities and speakers, and then there was a chance to address them by video. People loved them and it became a memorable way of connecting with the entire team. Do town halls as often as you can. Use technology like an intranet, but make sure you have ambassadors inside the business who leverage the messaging.

Your personal risk grows significantly because in the beginning you might be responsible for ten people, fifteen people, twenty people, and you know them all. Then, suddenly, you're responsible for a thousand people, and you only know a few. Actually, all of them have signed a contract with your company and expect your company to help them grow their careers, offer them great opportunities to deliver great work, and provide a great atmosphere with great colleagues, ideally with clients that are demanding, challenging, but also inspiring.

Read the signs very, very clearly when you come into any office that you have to work in or visit. Notice how people look at you and whether they welcome you with open eyes, or whether they just look to the side and walk away or walk past you. You have to develop a bit of a radar for the atmosphere and the intangible qualities of what temperature your organization has.

When you're at that point, the best thing that can happen to you is to have people that you can trust in your closest leadership circle. You can talk to them and involve them in how you deal with certain things. That obviously takes a lot of the weight off of you, and makes them part of the real leadership team of the company.

WALKING THE WALK

There are two things that define knowing what's important to running firms. Your primary job is your belief in your role, and how extraordinary and challenging it might seem for some to move from an operational role into one that you immediately defined as being a keeper of a belief system. Be a keeper of a belief system, and a propagation communicator, as well as someone who lives out what they believe and demonstrates that "I'm not an exception to our values." I have lived in organizations that set out separate rules of behavior: one for their employees and another for leadership. I always felt this was the worst sort of leadership behavior. (It gives leadership a bad name.) Your people always have an eye on you, especially when things aren't going well. I know that no matter what happens, I made sure that I exercised a certain confident calmness. They would always get the same kind of steady "It's going to be fine. It's going to be great." Just keep your nose down and keep going.

YOUR EXIT

At some point you will exit. I know for some of you reading this, it seems a preposterous notion as you're knee-deep in growing your company and focusing on the endless list of things that need to get done. It is a reality that every chief executive should be thinking about and planning carefully for. It is pretty obvious that succession planning is vitally important to the health of the company, and yet in my experience it's something that is not always well planned for. The successor need not be a carbon copy of you, as the era that the company find itself in will no doubt need some skills which you have and others you don't. What is important is that the person that you seek is compatible with the values of the company. They may have a very different view of how to do things, but there can be no doubt as to their abiding belief in what the company that they are joining stands for.

Remember Chapter 1—obviously, I had the privilege of being the second-generation CEO. When Steve retired, I was committed to ensuring that his departure was celebrated in a very special way and that all the key people who were part of the journey up to his departure had an opportunity to wish him well personally. I imagined how tough it must have been to hand over the leadership of something you built yourself. And it was not easy. But the way the leadership team gave Steve a "farewell and thank you" during his last days in the business is something he will always remember.

The question as you exit is, what kind of "leaver" will you be? What is remarkable is that each person leaves the role that has been such an integral part of their life in different and distinct ways. How you choose to leave the firm will be a part of the legacy you leave behind and the life that you live going forward. To help you reflect on this reality, let me introduce you to four different personalities and the way they leave their positions, for better . . . or for worse. They are the Coach, the Professor, the Adventurer, and the Emperor.

THE COACH

The coach becomes a contributor, advisor, and "chairman emeritus" of the company. You give over the reins of power to become a supportive advisor and an endless resource for perspective, guidance, and team confidence. It is a wonderful role, where you can revel in the growth of the people you have put in place but also enjoy the fruits of all of your labor, while feeling valued and cherished as a part of the company that you worked so hard to create and grow. You don't have to maintain a physical presence any longer, and what's great about this role is it allows you to stay involved with something that is such a part of you. The entire organization sees you as still an important part of the firm, a person who offers unconditional support and approval coupled with wise and generous counsel. There is a catch, though. The only way this can happen is if you have the confidence and the wherewithal to *let go*.

THE PROFESSOR

You might not want to be involved in your company directly anymore and yet you still love the industry, so you might wish to develop a broader industry presence, building on your experience to become a bit of a guru for the industry that you enjoyed for so many years. There are loads of opportunities where you can contribute via associations and other industry bodies. One thing to reflect on is, "Well, what was my net contribution and what is my core and essence and how might I share that with the industry at large?" It's a challenging thing to do when for so many years your identity was printed on a business card and now you are another outside expert. Discovering it is a journey in and of itself. Reach out to others to help you with that reflection. It's fun, it's liberating, and I think it's something that many of us can look forward to.

THE EMPEROR

Many executives leave the firm that they founded and grew, go to the goodbye party, and take their gold watch, while all the while, plotting their return. (Napoleon comes to mind.) For many of these people, the notion of them not being at the helm of the company, controlling events, is utterly unthinkable. While they will depart, they will not go quietly into that good night. I have seen this again and again where individuals simply were not able to evolve their self-identity into something that was not inextricably attached to the company they founded. It is sad for the person who is struggling to develop an identity outside of the company but even more challenging for the people who now run the firm and seek their own sense of identity and future for the organization. Beware of Napoleons!

THE ADVENTURER

For many, life is lived as a series of chapters. For them the adventure of starting and growing a company is but one phase in a sequential series of exciting life experiences. It's a personal choice, and if you're thinking about it as you read this, I wish you well in the search for your new chapter. It is possible that the departure from the role of founder and chief executive is a complete break, where you evolve into a new phase of your life having nothing to do with your previous time as entrepreneur and company growth agent. I know many of these people, and they are delirious about the new chapters in their lives and they haven't looked back. Who knows, maybe this is you?

HOPE AND A PROMISE

I wrestled with a number of ways to conclude my thoughts for you. How could I summarize what I think a CEO's role is, what to promise your people, and what to dedicate yourself to? Then it hit me: the note I sent my people when I took the reins of the company. I have taken a few items out that would not mean much to you (!) and share here the essence of what I believed then and I deeply believe now:

> Dear all,
>
> I write to you in my new role as the chief executive officer of Spark44. I suppose this is different than most CEO appointments, where often a new person from the outside is selected, a stranger to the company and a person whose values and intentions are not yet understood. But in true Spark44 manner we have taken a different approach. I would like to take this opportunity to share my values and intentions with you today—reminding many of you who know me personally, as well as providing an insight to those that I have not had the opportunity to speak with on a one-to-one level yet, of what they are.
>
> Steve, and all the founders, have been busy with what I call the era of designing Spark44. He envisioned a company—a place—that everybody wants to come to every day, where good work is encouraged, recognized, and fought for. I can confidently say, we are that place—and we will remain being that.
>
> It has been an amazing achievement to design and implement a worldwide network of talent to propel at first the Jaguar business and subsequently Land Rover. We delivered a proof of concept demonstrating that what we have created works—ultimately, we have proven that this construct is unique, its achievements clear and meaningful and everything we have done for these two clients is vitally important to their success—in a very discrete way for Spark44.
>
> Now is the time to build on this. In my words: we are now entering the era of recognition.

If the era of design was about a different kind of company, the era of recognition will now start because we are a different kind of company. There is no other place that drives communications through all touchpoints in such a seamless way. Our values remain our cornerstone, but we need to reimagine them in this context:

We must continue to be bold but now think big and dare to pursue greatness.

We must be brave—to be courageous in undertaking the difficult and arduous process of actually making greatness happen.

We must be honest to challenge any convention, to challenge any previous wisdom, to confront any naysayer and any force that stands in the way of greatness.

Now as your new CEO there are two important questions:

What do I believe?

Of course, I share deeply the values of being bold, brave, and honest but there are some other things I believe that some of you may know, but certainly all will come to know:

I believe everyone deserves a place at the table.

Diversity and inclusion are what make a high-performing company. We will be celebrated across the industry for this vitally important cultural requirement.

I believe everyone must be heard.

For good or for bad we will either succeed or fail to the degree to which our people feel free and the mechanisms exist both to innovate but also to critique, to challenge, and to share their views on what may be restricting or supporting progress toward the achievement of greatness.

I believe we must take more risks.

Client service must not be defined as servitude. It must mean challenging our clients and bringing them new and expansive means of advancing their fortunes. It is all about not what is requested but what is required.

I believe we must decentralize innovation.

I want a culture of experimentation where greatness is created not as a top-down affair but in all corners of the company big or small and where people feel unfettered permission to create something great.

And, finally, what will I do?

There are many ways to define the chief executive job. My task will be to drive the recognition of the greatness. I will be its coach, champion, leader, curator, and salesman. For me, a contemporary chief executive is a change agent, and I intend to set my sights accordingly. Everything I will do will connect to our "WHY"—as in empowering people to challenge conventions so that amazing things happen.

I will be challenging the status quo both inside our company and for the way our client does business.

I will be a champion of great ideas, great thinking, and great innovation. I have a duty to see to it that the greatness that our organization creates and the individuals themselves are able to innovate without interference and to allow their innovations to blossom.

I will be a keeper of the culture. I will find means to make being bold, being brave, and being honest a practical reality and to live in meaningful ways in all corners of our company—speaking with each other and not about each other.

I will be a nurturer of talent. I believe my primary task is to attract but, most importantly, to nurture and retain the people of our company to see to it that they are inspired, encouraged, and that they are equipped to be every possible best that they can be.

I will look at the horizon exploring what greatness will continue to mean both for our company and for the industry at large.

I will be the chief growth agent for our company, bringing new partners and new opportunities for all of you.

So, we are on a journey. And like with any journey, you pack for the trip. For us there are some things we will be taking with us for certain and other things we will decide to leave behind.

We take with us our culture and what it is we value.

We take with us our belief and support for one another as an interdependent whole.

We take with us the confidence in our ability to achieve greatness.

We leave behind any separation of one another by location, group, or discipline.

We leave behind any inkling of subservience to any person or entity either inside or outside of our company.

We leave behind any structure and process that gets in the way of our ability to innovate.

Now is the time to embark. I need all of you to know now where we are going, what you can expect of me and certainly what I will be expecting of you. I invite you to help Spark44 make history for a second time—a history of recognition of industry greatness.

I believe at the end of the day our greatest work is yet to come, so let's go to work.

Ralf

Ralf Specht
CEO, Spark44

Checking the List

✓	Have you institutionalized *culture, relationship, protection,* and *direction*?
✓	Do you have a regular way to communicate with your leadership and people?
✓	How do you manage the balance of *challenge* and *support*?
✓	Have you reflected on what type of a personality you want to be when you have exited?
✓	Do you have a sounding board that ensures your exit is perceived the way you intend?

AFTERWORD

IT'S ALL ABOUT THE PEOPLE

THEY MADE AND MAKE THE DIFFERENCE

"In the early days I knew everyone at Spark44."

"Now is the time to thank everyone for their contribution—the ones that started on day one as well as the ones who just joined recently."

Creating a global company in record time and scaling it to a size of fourteen times the day one staff in an organic fashion is an undertaking that no one that has been part of it will ever forget. The values that drove this growth and the reputation for excellent marketing communications programs that were created with our client partners were two key pillars on which Spark44 was built. We always put the quality of work and the quality of talent at an equal level.

From the initial offices in Los Angeles, London, Frankfurt, and our partner agency DMG in Shanghai, through to our next phase of the Spark44 offices in Shanghai, Birmingham, and Sydney, up to the 2015 expansion into Sao Paulo with our partner agency Babel, and to Moscow with our partners from Albion to our owned offices in Madrid and Rome, Mumbai, Johannesburg, Dubai, Singapore, Seoul, Tokyo, New York, and our latest growth into Bogota and Taipei: without the knowledge and expertise, the dedication and passion of hundreds of people, we would not have been able to build Spark44.

It's fair to say that in the early days our processes were manual and not digital; we're also no longer permitted to retain records beyond a particular timeframe, which means there was no way to get in touch with all of you—I would have loved to include all of your names here, but legally that is unfortunately not possible. Consider yourselves mentioned here. In the book I could only mention a few—but none of them could have done what they did without your energy, passion, and desire to be part of something unique. A business model that in our industry was considered revolutionary made it a continuous target both of colleagues who wanted to join and other agencies who wanted to learn from it.

Before I close this book, I have to mention the "real boss"—my assistant Jane Hois, who has been working with me from day minus-thirty at Spark44—the days before we even had an office and were sharing workspaces with other agencies we were friends with. I would not have been able to manage the organizational load that comes with such a huge organization without her—and without the trust that I put into her in managing the daily life behind the scenes. Her calm and considered approach, paired with an eye for everything that could make her colleagues' lives easier, was something that made her famous in our company the world over. She organized all of our Finca Meetings and ensured that everything that was not planned never felt as if it wasn't—and she did all of it with a smile.

Thank you.

P.S.: The manuscript for this book was finalized in November 2019; ironically, only just days before my sudden departure as CEO. It was not possible to publish the book in 2020 as initially planned and I have to deeply thank the team at Radius Book Group with Scott Waxman, Mark Fretz, and Evan Phail for their support and understanding about the delay. You guys have been awesome.

P.P.S.: Between December 2019 and the summer of 2021 many colleagues who were aware of the book project asked me whether the book would finally be published and whether it would include a chapter about what happened after my departure. I decided not to include anything about the events of 2020 and 2021 except for one comment I received in May 2021 from Antonella Cesta, the account director from our Rome office who had started with us back in 2012. Antonella always had her heart in the right place, and her words speak for themselves: "This is the end . . . at the end . . ."

ACKNOWLEDGMENTS

THERE IS NO BUSINESS WITHOUT A CLIENT

"Are the guys in headquarters crazy?"

"We have a choice to run with it and make it work or not."

These thoughts that the Spanish Brand Director Oscar Oñate shared with me while we were busy setting up new offices back in spring 2015 are ones I will never forget. He put in words what many might have thought, and not everyone had come to the same conclusion. A few of Oscar's colleagues are mentioned in these ten chapters. But there are many more who deserve to be named; I hope I have not forgotten anyone:

Bernard Kuhnt and Wolfgang Ungerer in Europe, who committed to the startup in 2011 in a way that was significant and allowed the European teams to get off to a good start.

Chris Wilde, who saw the opportunity Spark44 would bring to their overseas markets and supported the setup across the world.

Daniele Maver, Marco Santucci, and Fabiano Romano in Italy with their continuous focus to do the right thing.

Luis Ruiz and Oscar Oñate, who supported our vision of a fully integrated agency with dedication and passion that was second to none.

Andy Goss and David Pryor in the USA, who challenged for breakthrough work in the US and supported from the heart.

Victoria Morris at headquarters—without her dedication in the early days we would not have been able to set up an operational basis that was delivering what was really needed.

Barry Carsley, who joined our JV board as an observer from the get-go and has been a thoughtful and wise challenger to both us and his internal colleagues whenever it mattered.

Ian Armstrong, who wrote the foreword and whose focus has always been the greatness of the output for the two iconic brands.

Eric Labourier and Andy Parker—both gentlemen were critical to making great work happen.

Glyn Butterworth, without whom the transition of more than 60 accounts globally in 2015 would not have been possible.

Anthony Bradbury, who was on our side during and after the integration of the Land Rover accounts globally with an unmatched sense of managing the internal stakeholders.

Rohit Suhri, who runs the India JLR operations and has provided wisdom along the way and support throughout.

Bruce Robertson, initially in Shanghai and later in Dubai, who probably saw the value of the approach more than many others.

Hannah Naji, who was our key client in the Middle East, and actually struck the perfect balance between challenging and supporting our teams.

Lisa Mallett in South Africa, who was brave enough to hear out all the challenges and committed to the most significant team turnaround of all our market relationships.

Steven de Ploey, first at headquarters and then later in France, who always focused on the "art of the possible."

Tim Howard, who has been a voice of reason when it was necessary.

Hans Riedel, our first chairman, who made his dream of founding an advertising agency come true more than forty years after he had left Young & Rubicam Frankfurt and become the premium car guy whose reputation is unparalleled across the world.

REST IN PEACE

Much too early, my fellow board member Alistair Cook passed away in December 2020. Chapter 7 shares his significant contribution as Chief Financial Officer to Spark44. When I invited him to our Finca session in Italy in 2018, our entire team wore Scottish rugby shirts paying tribute to his legacy. My speech focused on what his time with us meant for the people at Spark44: "Alistair cared. He took care. Not just of the finances. Alistair always knew that numbers are the consequence of people's behaviors. People mattered to Alistair . . . and for many he had become the voice of wisdom over the years . . . people knew they could trust him and that his word mattered . . . when they were seeking advice or just wanted an open ear."

A few months later in March 2021 Aditya Atri passed away, too. Aditya was key to our growth in Mumbai during the transition of the Land Rover accounts into our developing agency back in 2015. Another true gentleman who left us way too early.

GREAT READINGS

INSPIRATION AND DIRECTION ARE OFTEN FOUND IN SPECIAL PLACES

"Guys, you got to read this book. It looks at other sectors—but the way the challenges are described makes me feel 'this could be us.'"

"Ralf, thanks for sharing that book. Now I understand why they behave the way they do. I wish I had known earlier, would have made many things easier."

Greg McKeown, *Essentialism—The Disciplined Pursuit of Less* (Crown Business, ISBN: 978-0-7535-5516-3). Greg was the keynote speaker at our first Finca Session after we had grown by twelve offices in six months. We had planned to do a two-hour keynote and discussion—and it became a five-hour intense discussion about what would be essential for us as a business and our leaders as we would embark on an exciting journey.

Chris Zook and James Allen, *The Founder's Mentality* (Harvard Business Review Press, ISBN: 978-1-63369-116-2). When the company had grown by a factor of three within six months, the growing pains were becoming obvious, and with them the growing sense that we might be losing something. This book by Bain & Company consultants Chris Zook and James Allen helped us understand what we were up against and how we could overcome some of the challenges we were facing.

Captain D. Michael Abrashoff, *It's Your Ship: Managing Techniques from the Best Damn Ship in the Navy* (Grand Central Publishing, ISBN: 978-1-4555-2302-3). With new executive leaders coming into the business and great talent from within becoming managing directors we gave this book away. A fascinating story about a turnaround based on values. Good read when things are broken—but also when you feel you have got to do something now in order for things not to break.

Simon Sinek, *Start with Why* (Portfolio Penguin, ISBN: 978-1-59184-644-4). Twelve months into being a company of 900 staff after previously having only been 250, the question that was heavily debated was what is our "why." Many had read Simon's book—so we reached out to him and he sent Peter Docker, who facilitated to identify our "why" at our 2017 Finca in Sinzig near Cologne, Germany. A very inspiring book and a great methodology. Peter got so many great stories from the sixty of us at the workshop that we decided to do a little internal book called *Spark-Life—The Stories So Far*.

Peter Block, *The Empowered Manager* (Wiley, ISBN: 978-1-119-28240-2). Our Larry evaluation methodology included a section on empathy. When I was wandering through a Barnes & Noble bookstore in New York I got hold of this book, read it, and then ordered a few for my executive colleagues. Steve called me up afterward and said, "Now I understand why they behave the way they do. I wish I had known earlier, would have made many things easier." It's all about positive political skills at work.

Jeff Haden, *The Motivation Myth* (Portfolio Penguin, ISBN: 978-0-399-56376-8). What's the secret behind motivation? Jeff's book speaks about "how high achievers really set themselves up to win," which is something everybody experiences during their career. But when you are leading a company, you'd better understand the theory behind it because every now and then you have to deal with it. When I shared that book at our Sonning Finca, in 2018 some of my executive colleagues thought it was a bit banal. Well, interestingly they figured out shortly after that it was anything but banal.

Kevin Allen, *The Hidden Agenda* (Bibliomotion, ISBN: 978-1-937134-04-4). Kevin had been supporting us to sharpen our profile since 2013, so he was the perfect keynote speaker at our 2015 Kent Leadership Meeting—the last one before we invented Finca Sessions. His book is a great guide to the emotional dynamics and motivations that underlie every decision. Decoding them and understanding them is of great benefit to everyone—not only in business.

When Ralf stepped down as CEO of Spark44, he received an overwhelming flood of messages that reminded him that the company he and his fellow cofounders built was much more than a global communications powerhouse, it was actually a company with soul. His book *Building Corporate Soul* reveals how true world-class companies create a culture that drive success with customers and resonates with employees and all other stakeholders.

Building Corporate Soul provides a unique framework (Soul System™) that aligns employee behaviors with corporate strategy via shared understanding and shared purpose. The Global Soul Index performance ranking demonstrates that companies that are operating within this framework outperform their peers significantly. It proves that the leadership behaviors that build soul *are* synonymous with the behaviors that build success.

Fast Company Press
Hardcover ISBN: 978-1-63908-002-1
eBook ISBN: 978-1-63908-003-8
Also available everywhere digital audiobooks are sold